SHAPING STRATEGY

Independent School
Planning in the '90s

SUSAN C. STONE

Design by Graphic Touch, Stoneham, Massachusetts

Second Printing 1996

Copyright © 1993 by the National Association of Independent Schools.

All rights reserved. No part of this publication may be reproduced in any form without permission in writing from the publisher, except by a reviewer who may quote brief passages in a review.

Printed in USA.

ISBN 0-934338-78-7

Table of Contents

Chapter One:	Planning in the 1990s	5
Chapter Two:	Preparing for a Planning Cycle	17
Chapter Three:	Strategic Thinking	38
Chapter Four:	Drafting the Strategic Plan	58
Chapter Five:	The Implementation Program	66
Chapter Six:	Appraisal and Revitalization	94
Chapter Seven:	Problems and Pitfalls	103
Afterword		115
Bibliography		117
Appendices		119

Introduction

One of the reasons that the very concept of "planning ahead" appeals to me is that it provides at least the illusion of some control over the future. Another is that the essence of planning is, and must be, dynamic. These essential points have led me to become a perennial student as well as a practitioner of the art of planning, of the endless variations on the basic theme.

I began as a volunteer what later turned into a full-time career. In the late 1970s I was asked as a trustee of Holland Hall School in Tulsa, Oklahoma, to chair the long range planning committee. My first reaction was to politely demur, explaining that I knew nothing of planning for an independent school – nor for anything else for that matter. When I was told that probably no one else did either, I accepted. "Little did I know..." as they say.

As part of my training I attended an NAIS-sponsored workshop for heads and trustees from a handful of schools. The purpose of the workshop was to share a model that had been developed by NAIS's Commission on Educational Issues.

Intrigued by what we learned there, we instituted the model at Holland Hall – and then received invitations to demonstrate it at several colleague schools in the Independent Schools Association of the Southwest. I began experimenting with ways to streamline the original model with other boards I served on, and was excited by both the reception and the results.

Early in the '80s I was asked at the last minute to fill in for an ailing member of the NAIS Trustee Committee at the annual school head/board chair workshop in Chicago. Following my presentation on long range planning (the accepted term at the time), I was deluged with requests for more details. John Bachman, an old friend and former Holland Hall faculty member, had just gone to work for NAIS. He asked if I would be interested in working with the organization to develop a project to respond to member schools' needs in the area of planning. I was indeed interested, made the first of many trips to Boston and logged the first of what were to become hundreds of thousands of frequent flyer miles to work directly with hundreds of independent schools.

We designed a project that focused on presenting a series of workshops sponsored by NAIS and regional associations to teach the evolving planning model to teams of trustees and heads who would then return to their schools armed with the how-to's of planning. I wrote a manual to explain the long range planning and policy development process, and we kicked off the series at the annual conference in Anaheim. We earnestly and, as it turned out, rather modestly estimated that we could reach a couple hundred schools and that the demand for planning services might last for two or perhaps even three years.

In fact, the initial results were: 18 workshops that took place over five years and reached about 600 schools; my book, *Strategic Planning for Independent Schools* (NAIS, 1987); an ongoing association with NAIS as strategic planning consultant; and a career that I had not planned until it took over my life.

Since my early taste of the process at Holland Hall I have studied a large number of the approaches to planning used by business, industry, higher education, and a variety of not-for-profit organizations. The majority of my clients (and those closest to my heart) are independent schools of all descriptions throughout the United States and in a few foreign countries. I have also served as a consultant to a cross-section of businesses, professional firms, economic development entities, charitable institutions, and professional and trade associations. All have given me invaluable insights into planning and wonderful opportunities to learn and to facilitate the process.

I continue to be involved in planning on the other side of the coin as a founding trustee of a publicly supported state magnet school, a trustee and advancement committee chair of an independent university, and as chair of the board at a large medical services/hospital complex. All are deeply engaged in strategic planning and all are grappling with vastly different sets of challenges.

The philosophy, concepts, and methodologies behind planning continue to fascinate me because the process is the exact opposite of static. Therefore, I'm always learning and adapting – which leads me to why I'm writing this book.

Literally the moment the ink was dry on my last book I wanted to say, "Wait! Here's another variation; it works fine to expand your planning team way past 12. Take into account *this* way to use data to help you make decisions," and so on. So when NAIS director of publications Catherine O'Neill called to tell me that the NAIS stock of *Strategic Planning for Independent Schools* was dwindling fast and asked if I would consider writing an update, I leapt at the chance. Having done so, I proceeded to procrastinate for some months, partly because I imagined that it would be relatively easy to write about what I love doing. It wasn't. Another challenge was the fact that many people have reported that they like *Strategic Planning* because it is simple, straightforward, and short. How to adequately represent all that I had learned since writing that book while maintaining the directness that made it useful was a time-consuming challenge.

Deadlines, ultimately, do arrive. With a lot of help from my friends, as the song goes, the update is in your hands. As you read it, highlight parts, make notes in the margins, agree or take exception, I hope you will find it to be a useful tool with many different applications. I offer my observations and thoughts as they have evolved and trust that you will see, as I do, that planning is not an event in and of itself, but a journey – and an exciting one at that!

Susan C. Stone
Tulsa, Oklahoma
January 1993

Chapter One
Planning in the 1990s

Volumes have been written in the past decade about effective planning. In this book, I propose to reexamine and update the process I described six years ago in *Strategic Planning for Independent Schools*. To analyze why that process has worked well in so many different kinds of schools, I surveyed current leadership and management literature about strategic planning. Many aspects of that research should be kept in mind as underpinnings for planning in the '90s.

A Matter of Vocabulary
The term "strategic planning," as strictly defined in the past, is out in many circles, according to J. Ian Morrison, President of the Institute for the Future in Menlo Park, California. "Strategy," however, is in.

According to Morrison, the technocratic strategic planning of the past, a process in which everything was analyzed and measured in great depth, is a dinosaur. The newly evolved, state-of-the-art planning is still strategic, but it has been adapted to include the following:

- It is linked to vision and mission – a simple clear, communicable description of an organization's future and why it exists.
- It employs environmental scanning techniques to help sort out what is really important as opposed to amassing vast quantities of documentation.
- It focuses on excellence, excludes the extraneous and emphasizes superb implementation.
- It mandates continuous flexibility as an imperative.
- It relies on simplicity, not jargon or a pretense of elaborateness. Although there will be complexity in context and content, the process itself must be simple.

Much of what I have observed and advocated for years is reflected in Morrison's views.

The process I described as "strategic planning and policy goal development" is necessarily conceptual and participatory. It revolves around creating a shared vision, developing a set of far-reaching goals, and designing a specific implementation and appraisal program for each goal. As defined, it is broad-brushed, creative and oriented toward a future that cannot be defined explicitly. "Long range planning" as such is operational and detailed; it explains how to reach specific goals that define overall institutional strategy.

The process is geared toward "policy goal development" because the resulting plan is initially developed as a set of recommendations to a school's board of trustees whose responsibility is at the policy level, not the operations level. The terminology was originated to avoid potential confusion between the role of the board and that of the administration and faculty in a school. However, as Richard P. Chait, Thomas P. Holland, and Barbara E.

Taylor write in *The Effective Board of Trustees*, a book based on their extensive research at the university level, "Trustees and presidents from almost all of the most effective boards emphasized that the board and other key stakeholders played integral and collaborative roles in the development of strategy." The authors then elaborate as follows: "However absorbed by such questions of strategy, effective boards did not allow themselves to become ensnared in the thickets of operational details." And, "... the effective boards we visited wanted and indeed insisted upon a level of participation that extended well beyond rapid yes-no decisions. Sensitive to academic protocol and reluctant to become enmeshed in administrative details, the attention of stronger boards was riveted on matters of overall corporate strategy."

First Steps
Regardless of the methodology you choose, the first step is to examine why your school should dedicate time and other resources to a planning process, even the most efficient of which will consume a fair amount of energy. The next step is to explore how to go about it.

The challenges of running an independent school become more complex with each passing year. Contributing to the complexity in an external environmental sense are changes in demographics, demands on families and, in turn, theirs on schools, the economic climate, opportunities and pitfalls inherent in technology, national educational reform initiatives, societal pressures, the prevailing political sentiments, the potential impact of a global society, and a host of other often bewildering issues. In a more local context for an individual school factors such as competition from other independent as well as public schools, shifts in the applicant pool, economic factors, governmental regulations affecting independent school operations, the availability of qualified teachers, transportation, the perception of and support for independent education, vying for limited philanthropic dollars, the cost of health care, and compensation levels in public school systems all contribute to the maze.

In his recent book, *The Art of the Long View*, Peter Schwartz quotes from "Historical Fact" by the French philosopher, Paul Valéry. "All the notions we thought solid, all the values of civilized life, all that made for stability in international relations, all that made for regularity in the economy... in a word, all that tended happily to limit the uncertainty of the morrow, all that gave nations and individuals some confidence in the morrow... all this seems badly compromised. I have consulted all the augurs I could find, of every species, and I have heard only vague words, contradictory prophecies, curiously feeble assurances. Never has humanity combined so much power with so much disorder, so much anxiety with so many playthings, so much knowledge with so much uncertainty."

These words seem as startlingly apt today as they must have seemed when written six decades ago. How then is a school to attempt to chart a prudent course, not only to survive, but also to thrive in the future?

Visions for the Future

Henry Mintzberg, Bronfman Professor of Management at McGill University and president of the Strategic Management Society, discusses his observations and theories about institutional planning in his book *Mintzberg on Management.* He maintains that "environments do not change on any regular or orderly basis. And they seldom undergo continuous dramatic change, claims about our 'age of discontinuity' and environmental 'turbulence' notwithstanding.... . The real challenge in crafting strategy lies in detecting the subtle discontinuities that may undermine an organization in the future.... . So the trick is to manage within a given strategic orientation most of the time yet be able to pick out the occasional discontinuity that matters."

At one time, the Greek military origins of the word "strategy" made me think that strategic planning would be an orderly process based on a rational analysis of strengths, weaknesses, and opportunities. It would produce focused, obvious strategies that would be recognized and willingly implemented throughout an organization. Mintzberg, however, prefers to think of strategy as *crafted* as opposed to *planned* in the military sense. He uses the metaphor of a potter creating a vessel from a mound of damp clay. Crafting strategy is achieved through skill, knowledge, experience, and commitment. He writes that, "The popular view is to see the strategist as a planner or as a visionary, someone sitting on a pedestal dictating brilliant strategies for everyone else to implement. While recognizing the importance of thinking ahead and especially of the need for creative vision in a prosaic world, I wish to propose an additional view of the strategist – as a pattern recognizer, a learner if you will, who manages a process in which strategies (and) visions can emerge as well as be deliberately conceived. I also wish to redefine that strategist, to replace that individual with a collective entity, made up of many actors whose interplay expresses an organization's mind."

Mintzberg makes it clear that strategic planning as such is dependent on both stability and on the mastery of details. The challenge then becomes not so much in promoting change, but in knowing when to do so. An obsession with change is dysfunctional; continuous reassessment of strategies can desensitize organizations to real change and render them inactive.

Both planning and crafting strategy are part of a process that I have come to characterize as "strategic thinking." Simply stated, strategic thinking combines both creative and analytic processes, leads to the definition of broad guidelines for future direction (both new and continuing), and to specific actions to implement and assess results.

How can an independent school look ahead to the puzzle of the future, determine where it may best capitalize on what it has been doing successfully, yet still respond to external pressures and competition? One answer is espoused by Peter Schwartz, a well-known futurist who is president of Global Business Network. Schwartz was a member of the group that revolutionized planning within Royal Dutch/Shell in the late '70s, a process that went on to overturn traditional concepts of planning throughout the corporate world. In *The Art of the Long View*, a fascinating book on his career, Schwartz explains that one of the best tools for helping individuals and organizations to consider the future is to create scenarios "... about the way the world might turn out tomorrow, stories that can help us recognize and adapt to changing aspects of our present environment. They form a method for articulating the different pathways that might exist for you tomorrow, and finding your appropriate movements down each of those possible paths. Scenario planning is about making choices *today* with an understanding of how they might turn out."

The entire process of planning should focus on making choices. For this planning process in independent schools, which have limitations of staff, resources, and time to devote purely to planning activities, I have developed an adaptation of Royal Dutch/Shell's scenario approach. In an era when an excellent independent school education is perceived in many sectors as less and less affordable, making strategic decisions based on a school's mission and educational priorities is essential for future viability.

Yet, Peter M. Senge, director of the Systems Thinking and Organizational Learning Program at MIT's Sloan School of Management, contends in his book, *The Fifth Discipline*, that most strategic planning is in reality reactive and relatively short-term. He has concluded that "It may simply not be possible to convince human beings rationally to take a long-term view. People do not focus on the long term because they *have* to but because they *want* to."

Planning activities in independent schools respond to both the *need* and the *desire* to engage in strategic thinking. The results tend to have implications for both the short and long term and in reality cannot be separated. One key is to develop a shared vision of a school that will animate not only the statement of its mission but also its future goals for all aspects of school operations.

Senge writes, "The origin of vision is much less important than the process by which it comes to be shared." Wherever he has seen "...a long-term view actually operating in human affairs, there is a long-term vision at work." In Senge's experience, which parallels mine, vision doesn't necessarily emanate from the top but often comes from individuals who are *not* in positions of authority. Organizational visions take time to emerge, and they tend to grow from the interactions of individual visions. "Experience suggests that visions that are genuinely shared require ongoing conversations where individuals not only feel free to express their dreams, but learn how to listen to each other's dreams. Out of this listening new insights into what is possible gradually emerge," Senge writes. Working with schools, I have observed repeatedly that it is the force of a truly shared vision that fuels the abstractions of a written plan, that ensures its vitality.

Senge considers a shared vision not merely an idea but "...a force in people's hearts." It creates "...a sense of commonality that permeates the organization and gives coherence to diverse activities... . One of the reasons people seek to build shared visions is their desire to be connected in an important undertaking... "

In subsequent chapters, I will discuss practical ways of recognizing and developing shared visions – keeping in mind that they are fragile and can dissipate or die prematurely. Senge lists several causes for this fragility. "Visions spread because of a reinforcing process of increasing clarity, enthusiasm, communication and commitment," he writes. "The visioning process can wither if, as more people get involved, the diversity of views dissipates focus and generates unmanageable conflicts."

According to Senge, the visioning process must involve inquiry, advocacy, and the ability of the organization to harmonize diverse views. The lack of these elements together will damage the shared vision as will the discouraging feeling that bringing it into reality is apparently too difficult, or if people become overwhelmed by the demands of current reality. And finally, "a vision can die if people forget their connection to one another. This is one of the reasons that approaching visioning as a joint inquiry is so important."

Senge thinks that to be really effective, there must be synergy between the vision, which is oriented toward the future, and systems thinking to reveal how what currently exists has been created. Mintzberg insists that the past, present, and future of any organization are inextricably linked. "Most of the time organizations pursue a given strategic orientation. Change may seem continuous, but it occurs in the context of that orientation and usually amounts to doing more of the same, perhaps better as well. Most organizations favor these periods of stability because they achieve success not by changing strategies but by exploiting the ones they have. They, like craftsmen, seek continuous improvement by using their distinctive competencies on established courses. While this goes on, however, the world continues to change, sometimes slowly, occasionally in dramatic shifts... . That long period of evolutionary change is suddenly punctuated by a brief bout of revolutionary turmoil in which the organization quickly alters many of its established patterns."

And what happens then? According to Mintzberg, "as an alternative to having to develop new strategies from scratch or having to import generic strategies from competitors, the organization can turn to its own emerging patterns to find its new orientation." My own experience has led me to see that most planning in independent is similarly evolutionary in nature.

The planning process described in this book is designed to help schools envision what they want to be – which in many instances is not very different from what they already are, although external factors can force sometimes dramatic alterations. The process aims to develop a mode of thought for considering alternatives, for playing "what if?" It also balances the creative scenario technique with analysis. It outlines ways in which a school can engage productively in strategic thinking – which in turn leads to strategic decisions supported by strategic programming and implementation.

As Senge writes, "Vision becomes a living force only when people truly believe they can shape their future." By its very definition, an independent school is in an almost ideal situation to articulate its vision and craft the strategy to achieve it, thus shaping its future. Hence the concept of *shaping strategy.*

What It Takes

In the chapters to follow, I will discuss the planning process, beginning with how to shape a plan that is a strategy for the future, and continuing with the realities of how to implement, update, and constantly renew it. I have found these themes to be consistent through all successful planning processes:

- They are based on broad participation, creating a shared vision and a sense of ownership.
- They provide for both creativity and analysis.
- Those who participate are sensitive to external, contextual factors and are aware of internal, institutional issues as well.
- The first product of the planning process is a series of strategies or goals for policy; the second is an implementation program.
- The focus is on the future rather than on defending or justifying past actions; it takes history and tradition into consideration, and remembers the lessons learned from them.
- The vision, mission, and goals derived from the process are seen as valid and consistent and have strong leadership support.
- The plan that grows out of the process is a concise, clear, written document that is essentially a framework for decision-making and shaping strategy.
- Throughout the active process and beyond there is deliberate communication among all the segments of a school's community about the process, the plan, and the expected outcomes.

An effective implementation program for the strategic framework

- is based on the discipline of a written plan, continually assessed and flexible
- assigns specific tasks to individuals, positions, committees or other identifiable entities
- delineates the locus for final authority, approval, and accountability for each action
- establishes realistic timelines in the short-, mid-, and long-term
- develops a consistent long-range financial plan to support the goals of the strategic plan
- incorporates a method for ongoing assessment of actual performance and for necessary corrective measures
- includes decisions made at the appropriate level that are based on solid data and information
- contains a clearly understood framework for appraisal of the strategic plan and updating the implementation program
- formalizes a systematic approach for continuous planning.

So much for theory. The following chapters will describe the practice of shaping, implementing, and renewing a strategic plan. For an outline of the process, please see Appendix A.

Chapter Two
Preparing for a Planning Cycle

Whether school leaders wish to develop a formal, written plan for the first time or update an existing one, there are a number of points to consider and issues to resolve in preparation for the process. You should:

- Design a planning approach and calendar that best suit the personality of a school and the expectations of members of the school community.
- Determine the size and composition of the planning team that will participate in the initial phases of the process.
- Choose appropriate leadership.
- Define the role of the head of school and the president of the board.
- Develop background data and resolve questions about the need for and the timing of detailed research, questionnaires, and focus groups.
- Figure out arrangements and logistics.

- Decide how and when to communicate throughout the school community.
- Think about managing the expectations that the process will raise in the school community.
- Consider flexibility and adaptability vs. process integrity.

This chapter will examine each item on this list in detail. Of course, since planning is a continuous, non-linear process, there will also be implications for each in subsequent chapters.

The Planning Approach and the Calendar
There are a variety of ways to structure a process while observing the tenets of good planning. Many schools choose to initiate the formal process with an intensive two- or three-day session following appropriate preparation. (I resist the practice of calling such a meeting a "retreat," opting instead for the term "workshop." A retreat calls to mind a quiet, contemplative setting with time for individual relaxation, reflection, and perhaps some team-building exercises. In a planning workshop there is plenty of team-building but it revolves around the work of strategic thinking, discussion, analysis, advocacy, and making choices. The head of one school remarked that instead of a "retreat" such an activity should be called a "forward.")

In a well-designed workshop there is ample time to raise questions, write scenarios, test for consensus, synthesize ideas, and build the skeleton of a report to a school's board. That preliminary report will consist of:

- the mission statement as accepted or with suggestions for changes
- a series of policy goals relating to major elements of a school's operations
- rationales and suggestions for implementation for each goal
- preliminary recommendations of strategic priorities

Following the workshop, a drafting team is charged with reviewing all the information generated in the workshop and editing a working draft for the participants' subsequent approval. The draft can be presented to the board for further discussion and any proposed changes. The board is asked to approve the mission and policy goals with the understanding that the suggestions for implementation are neither inclusive nor exclusive at this point in the process. The next step is the creation of the specific, sequential implementation program.

This approach works well in situations where relatively large numbers of people are involved as workshop participants and efficiency is essential; it generates enthusiasm and maintains momentum. It is also a good approach to use in updating an existing plan. However, it is important to note that a plan is not written in a two-day workshop. There is time for reflection during the drafting process and during communication with the school community that may be deemed necessary or prudent before finalizing the report of recommendations to the board. (Note that this approach assumes that major research and financial planning will be done as part of the implementation program.)

The sample calendar below is by far the most popular version with all types of schools:

Sample Strategic Planning Process
Suggested Calendar for Review and Discussion

Winter
  Preliminary planning
  Design planning process
  Complete list of 25-35 workshop participants
  Develop background data
  Communicate to the school community about the process
  Contact workshop participants
  Make logistical arrangements

Before Workshop
  Mail packets to participants to include cover letter, participant list, agenda, school data, succinct demographic data, mission statement, any relevant articles

March 5-7
  Strategic Planning Workshop
  Thursday evening, Friday, and Saturday
  (see sample agenda page 53)

Following Workshop
Type material developed at workshop

Designate members of a drafting team

Begin writing the draft of a report for the board

Second week of April
Disseminate draft to workshop participants for their review

April 22
Hold an editing meeting to incorporate comments as appropriate (allow time for a second meeting if needed)

Following editing meeting
Update draft

May 20
Present draft to board

Following board approval
Develop a specific implementation plan including a long range financial plan

Develop a regular appraisal mechanism

Implementation

Ongoing appraisal and planning

If people who are considered indispensable workshop participants are not available for a two- to three-day workshop, or if leadership thinks that what has been called the "blitz" approach doesn't fit current school needs and style, an alternative approach is to split those workshop days, scheduling them at workable intervals, perhaps with some homework assignments in between. This mode is exemplified by a calendar designed for Grace Church School, an elementary school in lower Manhattan, to update its six-year-old strategic plan:

Strategic Planning Process Calendar

Summer '91
    Preliminary planning

August 22
    Designing the process

Early September
    Finalize list of potential workshop participants

    Contact participants by letter, with follow-up phone calls as appropriate

    Develop data for background information

    Communicate to the school community about the planning process

October
    Complete data and any other relevant information for packets for participants

    Make final arrangements for workshop logistical support

First week in November
    Mail packets to participants, including cover letter, list of participants, agenda, data over a period of five years, summary of evaluation, summary of '84 plan, philosophy statement, any relevant articles

November 14-15
   Strategic Planning Workshop I (one and a half days; see sample agenda page 55)

November following Workshop
   Have material developed at the workshop typed and disseminate

November-January
   Task forces formed at workshop meet on their own two or three times to complete assigned tasks (each meeting should be limited to a couple of hours)

January 25
   Strategic Planning Workshop II (see sample agenda page 57)

January following Workshop
   Have information from workshop typed

February-March
   Begin writing a draft of the plan (drafting committee)
   Consult outside of drafting committee as needed
   Finalize draft

Late March/early April
   Disseminate draft to workshop participants for their review and red-penciling

April 9, late afternoon
   Editing meeting with workshop participants (two to three hours)

April/May
   Edit draft

Shaping Strategy

May 19
  Present draft to board

Following board approval
  Develop a specific implementation plan including a long-range financial plan

  Develop an appraisal mechanism

  Implementation

  Ongoing appraisal and planning

Variations are many, depending in some instances on whether surveys are to be done, focus group meetings are to be held, or on other needs specific to individual schools. In some schools there is an expectation that planning will follow a format that has been used before. Some schools choose to accomplish the work with a series of meetings rather than in one or two long workshops and spread the calendar over most of an academic year. This approach is used less and less, however. Whatever the reasons for choosing a particular format, you will improve your chances for success if you:

- ensure that there is a written calendar
- communicate to participants what is expected of them so they can make a commitment to participate on that basis
- clarify that the timing is realistic and will fit into the demands of the school schedule
- ascertain that the planning process will mesh with other major, time-consuming efforts such as a self-study for accreditation.

The Size of the Team

One of the primary principles in my philosophy of planning is that it be participatory. Members of the school community who merit inclusion in some fashion are (in no priority order):

- the board of trustees
- the school administrative team
- the parent body
- the alumni/ae
- the faculty
- the students

A special word about students: Often schools choose to seek ideas and responses from students within the general process by means other than including student representation directly on the planning team. Some of the reasons for doing so include concerns about asking students to give the amount of time needed, the sometimes potentially sensitive nature of questions to be raised, the feeling that students do not always have an overview of school operations and may tend to generalize from the specific (students are not, however, entirely alone in that trait), and in some schools, the fact that students are simply too young. But for a planning process to be truly participatory, students should be a part of the team. They see a school from a different and needed perspective, they can be a valuable liaison in the communication process, and they are, after all, a school's raison d'être.

If students aren't included directly on the planning team, their ideas can be solicited in various ways, such as from focus groups with student leaders, brainstorming sessions, and through creative writing projects. Their ideas can then be compiled for the planning team. An effective way to seek student ideas once the goal framework is in place is to ask for responses to specific goals and suggestions for implementation before decisions are made that would affect student life in the school; that information can be factored into the implementation program.

It can be helpful to include on the planning team people outside the school community itself, depending upon some of the challenges that may be seen to exist. Examples might include leaders from other educational institutions, civic leaders, and individuals who have specific information or perspectives to contribute. A participant from outside the school community may need a thorough briefing about the school in order to be able to contribute without feeling too much the stranger.

The size of a planning team is always a question – how to balance the need for inclusion with the limitations of effective group process. I have found that a representative team numbering between 28 and 35 people usually enables the inclusion of members of each of the school's constituencies and still promotes productive group process. I have worked with groups as large as 50. The trade-offs are for more involvement on one hand and for effective process on the other; it is sometimes more difficult to achieve consensus and begin to craft a coherent strategy the larger the team becomes. My general rule of thumb is to err on the side of inclusion rather than exclusion and then try to tailor the agenda to accommodate the group size.

Diversity of all kinds is desirable in a planning team. To achieve it a team is usually appointed by the head, board president, and planning process co-chairs. Some schools have found it politically useful to ask the faculty to elect from their ranks a designated number of team members or to nominate a list from which leadership can make final appointments. Representation from the faculty must be more than merely token.

There are schools that have asked all members of the board to be participants, recognizing that a board member may also be a parent or an alumnus. They then filled the remaining slots with key administrators and faculty members. This concept obviously depends on the size of the board and the desirable size of the planning team; it has been very productive for those schools.

One of the simplest ways to form a team is to simply list all ideal participants and then trim the list as practicality dictates. Some of the characteristics to consider in the potential members of a planning team include:

- a knowledge of and commitment to the school
- open-mindedness
- the inclination to listen to others
- tolerance for some ambiguity
- the ability to work comfortably within a group process
- an understanding of the role of questioning and consensus
- the willingness to commit the time required of team members to participate fully

Appropriate Leadership

Because planning is one of the fundamental responsibilities of a school's board of trustees, leadership for a process is often found at that level. The chair of the planning committee is a logical choice to be a co-chair for the process and the members of that committee are often the core of a planning team and serve as a steering committee within the process. Respecting the spirit of inclusiveness, asking someone from the school administration or faculty to fill the role of co-chair works well.

Head and Board President Roles

Each individual is vital to the process, but neither should assume a primary leadership role in the early phases of a cycle of planning. Both should certainly be members of the planning team. They will participate with the chair or co-chairs to designate team composition. The head will be heavily involved in helping to prepare for the formal process; however, since the philosophy is not to create a top-down approach, rather than occupying a dominant role, the head will simply be one member of the team during the strategic thinking phase, as will the board chair. The role for the head will increase following planning workshops, becoming even more visible in the drafting stage when the head will be the chief architect in designing the implementation program.

My description of the head's role as 1/32nd of a 32 person planning team has drawn fire from some quarters. I do not mean to imply that the head will abandon his or her institutional leadership role, or that a relatively new head should not articulate a strong future vision. Quite the contrary. Essentially, the question is "What if the head's vision is different from others'?" My response: If that is true, then the planning process provides an excellent forum for exploration, understanding, and resolution. Most heads anticipate such an opportunity with enthusiasm.

It has been said of leaders that they must be out in front, but not so far that the rest of us can't see them. Peter Senge writes of building a shared vision, one of the main points of planning, as follows: "Individuals do not sacrifice their personal interests in the larger team vision; rather the shared vision becomes an extension of their personal visions." I would suggest that the head's vision plays a significant part in animating a shared vision and that most school heads welcome the implicit mandate that results from such synergy.

Gary Benveniste supports the importance of such synergy in a discussion of what he terms "the multiplier effect" in his book *Mastering the Politics of Planning*. "The multiplier, an important concept in planning, refers to that moment in time when an idea catches on, where support for a new course of action multiplies, when indecision evaporates and individuals or groups decide to move ahead in a given direction." He continues, "The multiplier effect takes place when a shared belief emerges that this is the course to follow... or this is the policy to adopt or oppose." And, keeping the head's role in mind, "The multiplier is important because it is a source of power. When the multiplier operates, it becomes a force of shared belief that results in action."

Such momentum is precisely the desired outcome of strategic thinking. In an institution as intensely collegial as an independent school the head is not *solely* responsible for the vision of the school in the future; however, he or she is integral to the process.

If the head's view differs radically from everyone else's, in a healthy institution the effects must be faced. I would suggest that if such be the case, the differences will probably have surfaced before the planning cycle is begun.

The board president may be very active in the process while participating as a team member, then step back a bit in preparation for the fact that the first draft, when approved by the planning team, will be presented to the board for approval. There may be a role for the president as an advocate in preparing for the board presentation, or in keeping in touch with former board members or other key constituents as a courtesy to advise them of any critical recommendations. The president will probably be consulted with frequently during the design of the implementation program. There will undoubtedly be issues that surface during the process that directly affect the board, such as size, composition and diversity, committee structure, fundraising needs, communications issues, and policy questions. The president will take a role in resolving these issues, at the least to delegate responsibility for research and further recommendations to the full board for subsequent action.

Research

One of the most problematic aspects of a planning process is to assess adequately the need for data, deciding what will be actually useful and at what point it will be most needed. There are at least two schools of thought. The first is to recognize that the beginning of a new planning cycle is a relatively creative period of brainstorming external and internal issues, creating personal scenarios of the school in the future, raising questions, searching for consensus, and recognizing areas in which no consensus can be built. Therefore, school data developed for the planning team should be concise, focused, and limited basically to past performance, community demographic data, and perhaps some thought-provoking material such as trends in education and in independent schools, technology, and government regulations affecting independent schools at the federal, state, and local levels. These kinds of data and trend literature provide a picture of school operations from the past through the present, an assessment of where the school is now, and information to prime people's thinking in looking outside and ahead. Specific research, including surveying stakeholder groups, is then part of the implementation programming in response to the issues that have been identified in the planning process.

Richard C. Ireland, senior vice-president for strategic development at the Scripps Institutions of Medicine and Science, has wrestled with this question for years. He maintains that the more data we develop, the less we know. He places a high value on broadly derived and frequently gathered qualitative information, which makes any questionnaires developed much more effective. I have found that once issues are raised in a questionnaire, constituent expectations are also raised. I think it is the planning process to date that should set the agenda, not the framers of a questionnaire. Market surveys, whether conducted by the school or with outside help, are expensive and time-intensive and often provide more pertinent information when directed by the framework of the emerging plan rather than vice versa.

A second school of thought directs a school to engage the serious research described above during the preparation phase of a planning cycle *before* impaneling a planning team. Exigencies of budget, time, available personnel, how recently similar research has been done, and how the overall process has been envisioned will help each school to decide how to proceed.

An important caution is that research, analysis of data, and financial forecasting and planning techniques must come into play in making decisions for the future. The point is not whether they should be done, but when.

Aside from the question of how to approach research raised above, information that a planning team will find helpful includes:

- a copy of the current statement of mission and philosophy
- a copy of the last strategic or long range plan
- a summary of the report of the last accreditation visit, if recent
- budget results (in major categories)
- the tuition scale
- salary ranges
- the number of faculty members
- faculty-student ratio
- information on financial aid
- the size of the student body, the applicant pool, and numbers of students accepted and enrolled
- figures on student attrition
- significant changes in curriculum
- a list of the next level schools that graduates attend
- community demographics and economic indicators
- comparative data from peer independent schools and local public schools

Each school will compile data it considers relevant from the menu above and other items of particular significance. One caveat is that the data presented should be concise, compiled in graphs or a spreadsheet format, if possible, and constructed in a way that doesn't overwhelm people or focus their attention too specifically on numbers *per se*. Applicable data should be presented for a period of several years through the current year to display trends – and trends should be the focus of the data rather than single items. Some schools have elected to compile a five-year history, others have presented numbers at three- or five-year intervals to give an even longer period of comparison.

Where relevant, available data from local, regional or national peer group schools give a valuable frame of reference. National, regional, and city associations of independent schools are excellent sources of useful data.

Arrangements and Logistics
The planning effort will need various kinds of support. Secretarial assistance will be needed for correspondence with team members, helping to organize meeting arrangements, and typing the workshop results and iterations of the draft report. There will be budget items as well, mainly for postage, copying, meeting site expenses including refreshments and materials, and for consultant fees and expenses should outside assistance be deemed useful.

The site for a planning workshop is an important consideration. Holding extended meetings on campus can keep expenses down, focus attention on facilities, and ease gathering people together without travel time. Planning team expectations, and school tradition can also argue in favor of a campus-based meeting. On the other hand, a site other than the school gets faculty and staff away from on-campus demands, provides opportunities for social interaction in different surroundings, allows some distance and perspective on the subject, and highlights the special nature of the planning activity.

Schools have been very creative in finding places for planning workshops. Examples range from local hotels and conference centers to a working ranch in the Texas hill country, a spartan church retreat site, a trustee-owned hotel on a Florida beach, and a fishing camp on Squam Lake. (A "fishing camp" in New Hampshire has a vastly different connotation than the same in Oklahoma or Idaho.) The most successful sites are those that promote the work of the group. Some are sufficiently exotic to be distracting. In such cases planning team members might be invited to come before or stay after the sessions to enjoy golf, tennis, sailing, hiking and other local temptations to avoid real frustration.

Space needs will vary with planning team size; one space large enough for the whole team to convene, walls on which newsprint can be taped, and several spaces for small group discussions are the basic requirements.

Communication

Keeping the school community up to date on planning activities is an essential part of the planning philosophy. As preparations are made for beginning a new planning cycle, a communication schedule should be determined. Points to be communicated include: the process design and calendar; a list of planning team members; and the role the rest of the school community will be asked to play at what point in the process, i.e. responding to questionnaires or commenting in parent meetings or similar forums on recommendations that develop. Newsletter articles, pieces in alumni/ae publications, agenda items at meetings, and letters to parents all are convenient vehicles to keep people informed about the process and its outcomes. Keeping people informed is vital in preparing a foundation for change than may evolve from the process, and for major school-wide efforts, such as a curriculum reevaluation or a capital campaign, that may be cornerstones in realizing the vision. Because only a small proportion of the community will be directly involved in the process in the beginning phases, attention to good communication is an essential part of building support.

Germantown Academy, a Philadelphia-area coeducational day school of about 1000 students in grades PK-12, spread the word about its planning activities through a series of "town meetings" in coordination with undertaking the NAIS Multicultural Assessment Plan and other studies that were underway. When GA's planning team had completed its report to the board and received approval to develop an implementation program based on the proposed goals, the school sent a copy of the report with a cover letter asking for parents' responses before moving to the phase of delineating the implementation program. School leadership found that approach to communication very useful in promoting dialogue about issues and providing feedback about strategy. (Please see Germantown Academy's letter and other planning documents in Appendix B.)

The Hockaday School, a Dallas school for approximately 900 girls in grades PS-12, had recommended as part of its strategic plan a series of goals related to offering an innovative and stimulating curriculum: addressing moral, ethical, psychological, social and academic needs;

incorporating community, national and international affairs as a vital part of the academic environment; and encouraging the personal growth of the entire school constituency. The principal part of the supporting implementation program for the curricular goals was to engage in a large scale, two-year curriculum study. As the study began, every parent and faculty member was invited to attend one of a series of meetings in which the goals in the plan and the timetable for the curriculum study were presented. They were then assigned to small discussion groups and asked to brainstorm what they thought would be societal demands of their daughters, what they considered important in Hockaday's curriculum, and changes they would like to see incorporated. As a group they ranked each list. The information was compiled and provided to the curriculum study committee. Parents greatly appreciated being consulted and that pattern continued as the study developed.

Managing Expectations
Planning inevitably raises expectations – for additions to the curriculum (deletions are much harder for people to envision), for leading edge technology, for facilities, for increased faculty and staff compensation, for augmented library holdings, for lower student-teacher ratios, for enhanced financial aid... . The list is endless. At the same time, there is a sincere desire to keep tuitions affordable within the local or peer group market, concern about repeatedly going to parents for philanthropic support, pressure from competitive schools, a reported "austerity movement" in response to what has been viewed as the "excesses of the '80s," and the knowledge that a school cannot be all things to all people. A successful planning

process will lead people to make choices, to set priorities, and to recognize that planning is indeed for the long term. That the present school community holds the future in trust for future generations of young people is intrinsic to strategic planning. What is not realistic within the next three or five years may be quite possible in six years or ten if the foundation is solid. Shaping a strategic plan requires creativity, discipline, and clarity within the school community about institutional priorities, the various costs of trade-offs, and who will bear the burdens. The best way to manage expectations is to illuminate all of these issues clearly.

Flexibility vs. Integrity.
There are obviously many decisions to be made in tailoring the ideal planning process for a school. There is no one set method, no recipe that guarantees consistent results from school to school. However, observation of some of the basic elements of effective planning outlined herein, and examples of what has worked for a variety of schools will provide a toolbox from which a school can build a workable process. Planning is not a panacea; it is a highly useful management tool. A cycle of planning offers a school an excellent opportunity to educate members of its constituencies about the school and about some of the issues that may affect its future. It allows the school to arrive at a shared vision, to explore options and alternatives and, finally, to make informed choices according to its mission and priorities.

Chapter Three
Strategic Thinking

Following the preparation phase comes what I call "strategic thinking." The most efficient way to begin this phase is with a planning workshop. (Please refer to the planning calendar examples on pages 20 - 24.) Before the workshop, the planning format will have been set and scheduled, participants identified and notified, background data gathered and disseminated, the workshop site chosen, and specific agendas written.

The site should be conducive to comfortable working sessions, with a space large enough to accommodate all participants together, as well as breakout spaces for group discussions. The workshop produces a large number of newsprint sheets to be posted, so having walls on which newsprint can be taped is essential. Of course, as technology develops these may well become obsolete.

For the workshop you will need large newsprint pads, one or two flip charts or easels, felt-tip markers, and masking tape or other means to affix newsprint to walls.

Agenda points for a planning workshop include:

- introductions, process orientation, and review of background material
- brainstorming external factors that may affect the school
- brainstorming internal topics and issues to be considered in planning for the future
- responding to items on the brainstorming lists
- writing personal visions and scenarios
- synthesizing scenarios and testing for consensus
- drafting the policy goal framework
- appraising the mission statement
- establishing preliminary priorities
- assigning the work of the next steps in the process

There are advantages and disadvantages to holding a workshop on campus, off campus but still in town, or at a more remote site. The budget, participants' willingness to travel, and the appropriateness of available school facilities will all affect the decision. The choice should rest on the site where the team can be most productive, all things considered.

Orientation and Review

The opening session of the planning workshop facilitates group interaction and addresses the context for the work to follow. Holding it in the evening with a light supper is a pleasant way to begin, whether on campus or at a conference center or "retreat" site. Giving participants an opportunity to understand how the planning process has been designed and to question and discuss the background material is the primary purpose of the evening, in addition to allowing for some "social time" for informal conversation and getting to know members of the team.

External Factors

Brainstorming external trends and issues such as those relating to economics, politics, education, technology, demographics, psychographics, and societal mores and values helps team members begin to engage in strategic thinking. The purpose of brainstorming is to develop in a non-critical manner a wide-ranging list of signposts to the future in a short period of time. Discussion and exploration will come later. Brainstorming encourages participation by all members of the group, and begins to bring to light people's interests and concerns. Context is vital for strategic thinking and planning; external events and trends are driving forces that can have a profound effect on a school over time.

Brainstorming external factors should include those of international and national significance as well as those of regional and local importance.

The rules for brainstorming are simple:

- All ideas should be shared regardless of their seeming unimportance or whimsicality.
- Ideas should be brief and concise.
- Repetition and "piggybacking" are acceptable.
- Evaluation, criticism, and discussion are not allowed.

Team leaders will need to keep the pace rapid, record responses on newsprint and post them, enforce the rules, and ensure that one or two vocal individuals don't dominate.

Internal Issues
The technique employed for looking externally is repeated for airing institutional items that team members think should be addressed during this round of planning. External factors are outside the control of any member of the team; internal ones are not, and may potentially be turf-threatening. Therefore, it is essential that the *spirit* of brainstorming be preserved, and the team be reminded that the list is not intended to represent consensus at this point. Although the team is restrained from evaluation and discussion during brainstorming, those processes will become the rule as the workshop unfolds. If a team member disagrees with an item listed, he or she is free to propose something different.

General categories into which most internal brainstorming fall are:

- program (curricular and extra- or co-curricular)
- faculty
- students
- parents and families
- alumni/ae
- administration and staff
- physical plant
- finance and development
- marketing and public relations
- governance

The brainstorming lists begin the itemizing of the issues around which strategy will ultimately be formulated. It is not uncommon for planning teams to list page after page after page of items. Some people will think the team has opened far more doors than it can possibly close, but closure is the opposite of the purpose of brainstorming. In some ways, the brainstorming serves as what I consider to be a positive grievance session; there is ample opportunity for people to say what is important to them and have it noted. Some of those comments will be material to planning for the future; others will not. Some will be very short term, problem-solving points with little to do with strategy; others will be philosophical, conceptual, essential for shaping strategy considerations. It may prove difficult for the school head or others in leadership positions not to feel a bit defensive during a brainstorming session, but it is a valuable part of team building. Planning is a winnowing process, too. Those items that are not perceived by a large part of the team as germane will "disappear" as chaff from grain.

Responding to Brainstorming

If there is sufficient time, one way in which to invite the team to respond to the brainstorming lists is to cluster related items, as in the categories listed above, and then ask for ways in which the school might respond over time. It is often hard for some individuals to be open-minded about some of the contributions of their colleagues. For instance, faculty members who feel stretched to their personal and professional limits may quail at suggestions of a longer school day, year-round school, adding to the curriculum, or asking faculty to assume counseling roles in addition to all those they already perform. A comforting reminder is that it must not be assumed that the program of the future will be performed by existing personnel, or within today's perceived constraints. Brainstorming, particularly about school issues, must be done in the atmosphere of what Coleridge described as "the willing suspension of disbelief." Otherwise, planning gets out of the realm of strategic thinking and into the realm of immediate problem-solving.

In responding to ideas, the brainstormed contributions should begin with *verbs* to indicate what actions might be; otherwise there is a tendency just to repeat the issues, rather than consider what could be done about them.

Shaping Strategy

At Manzano Day School, an elementary school in Albuquerque whose physical heart is a 17th-century hacienda listed on the National Historic Register, a number of issues brainstormed in a 1984 planning workshop related to plant needs. This is how the participants described what they needed to do:

- Create and maintain green spaces – a feeling of an urban oasis.
- Continue to improve buildings to suit and support the academic program and accomodate growth.
- Ensure that any building or renavations are in keeping with the ambience of the present campus.
- Develop the Fenton Ranch property for an outdoor curriculum / summer program.
- Design a master plan to include expansion into adjacent buildings we don't own now.

The responses all begin with verbs. Some might be discarded, others given thorough consideration, still others eventually implemented. (A visit to Manzano eight years after the session at which these example ideas were listed confirmed that all of the plans had been accomplished. Reported the head, "Writing a good idea into the plan was tantamount to achieving it!")

Personal Visions and Scenarios

If there is not time to systematically brainstorm responses, another form of response is to write individual scenarios. Each team member writes a personal vision, a scenario for the school in the future. Instructions for scenario-writing are first to write a succinct vision of the school, literally an image of what the person would like to see or find on returning to the school in ten years. A scenario should be sited comfortably in the future so that the writer may get beyond defensiveness about current operations or personalities.

One way in which to defuse or de-escalate short-term issues is to look at them in the long term. I have found that people can talk about the future in a much less contentious way than about the present – and issues are still addressed. In addition, if asked to write a scenario three or five years into the future, the horizon is just too limited and there are simply too many inhibitors for thinking creatively. Writing a scenario is not creating a picture of a perfect school in a utopian future; it is a fine balance between the art of the possible and the reality of the probable, between dreaming and limiting circumstances.

Next, the scenario writer will address each of the main categories into which the internal brainstorming lists were grouped and list important objectives within each. Scenarios should be written with external trends and issues as a backdrop for the writer's description of the future school.

A scenario is broad-brushed and oriented 10 or more years into the future. The eventual strategic plan may not be valid for 10 or more years, but beginning the process by taking the long view is absolutely essential. Scenarios are stories that illuminate the way people *see* and *feel* about the school in the future as well as how they *think* about it. A scenario could take hours to write; within the planning workshop there is much less time, perhaps an hour at most. That tends to be sufficient for people to get their most cherished ideas on paper.

Synthesis and Consensus

Dividing the team into small discussion groups to hear and compare what people have written begins the process of synthesizing personal scenarios to test for consensus, or to try to build it if there are differences of opinion about major directions. Team members must differentiate here between ultimate goals and the variety of ways to realize them. The tasks at this point are to sort out the themes that are common to the small group's scenarios and identify questions that may not be amenable to resolution within the group. Drafting goal statements follows after the entire team has heard all the small group presentations. Each discussion group is directed to write the basic elements of its combined scenarios on newsprint for presentation to the team, highlighting the areas of consensus and those in which consensus was not achieved.

The artful division of the planning team into small groups of five to seven members to compare and contrast personal scenarios will help balance personalities and gender, and ensures a diversity of positions, constituency representation, and viewpoints for each of the groups.

Policy Goal Framework

Following the presentations of the discussion groups the common emerging themes can be molded into policy goals. Policy goals are positive, comprehensive statements of future direction, in effect recommendations of strategy for the board's consideration. Each goal statement will be supported by a rationale and a list of suggestions for implementation. At this stage these suggestions are neither inclusive or exclusive, but illustrate what actions must be explored and what decisions must be made and implemented to achieve the goals. The policy goal statements will be valid for years; they are umbrella statements for the more specific implementation suggestions, short-, mid- and long-term. The latter will be adjusted constantly.

The scenario discussions produce an abundance of reasons why the goals are central to the future, as well as a wealth of suggestions as to how the goals might be implemented. Building on these blocks to compose a draft of the policy goal component of the plan is the next step.

To continue the spirit of participation and the emerging sense of ownership it is a good idea to use the team to write a first draft of the goals, rationales, and suggestions for implementation during the planning workshop. One method is to divide the team into new small groups and assign to each one of the goal topic areas derived from the small group presentations. For example, if there are to be goals in each of the categories of program, students, faculty, etc., one group of several people would be asked to work with the material presented by the discussion groups related to program, another with faculty, another with students, and so on. Each would analyze what the previous discussion group reported to the full group about its assigned topic and extrapolate to propose a policy goal section as described. Examples of policy goal sections from several schools' completed plans are found in the Appendices.

If there is not adequate time allotted in the workshop for the team to develop the skeleton draft of the policy goal sections, it can be delegated to a drafting group and brought back at a later time for the team's editing. (See the process calendar for Grace Church School on page 22.)

The Mission Statement

The mission statement is preeminent in the hierarchy of a strategic plan. The reason that I suggest providing a copy with the background information, reviewing it at the opening planning session, and then not focusing on it formally again until after developing the preliminary draft of the policy goals is threefold. The first reason is to avoid limiting perceptions of the school's purpose in the future. In order to have the power to shape the future, a planning team shouldn't be constrained in envisioning it. I have found that few schools actually change their fundamental mission dramatically. However, schools frequently do come to perceive their mission somewhat differently and redefine it according to the insights gleaned in the planning process. Often the existing statement seems generic; that realization leads to careful revisions and sometimes to a total overhaul of a statement in which the language is too broad or the concepts are outdated. There is a lot of pressure on a mission *statement* – but a restatement doesn't necessarily mean a school's *mission* has altered.

Second, there are those who would argue that a school can't plan strategically without a mission statement that is generally supported. I agree; as described earlier, this process begins with reviewing the existing mission statement. One view of a planning process is that it is all essentially an appraisal of the mission to determine whether it will serve in the future as it has in the past. Some schools find that their mission and the manner in which it is stated can remain unchanged for decades.

The third reason for delaying a formal examination of the mission statement until after the preliminary draft of the policy goal sections has been completed is to make the discussion more efficient. Anyone who has spent time in mission statement deliberations knows that they often focus on semantics and can continue for hours, not always productively. The formal examination of a school's mission statement within the planning process is much more productive if it is not engaged prematurely.

A mission is the servant of the broader vision; often both are articulated in the same statement. One of the reasons that independent school missions don't seem to change drastically over time is that they represent an initial coalescence of the values of the founders of a school, supported subsequently by people of like mind who were attracted to the school, and then reinforced by procedures, traditions, beliefs, behaviors, and a successful history. All of this strengthens the sense of mission that is unique to a school, but not necessarily unique among all schools. The people who associate with a school tend to do so because they share similar beliefs and values; such association is not random.

The mission is a statement of why a school exists, frequently followed by a more explicit statement of educational philosophy. There are those who insist that a mission should be expressed in only one sentence (next to impossible for most schools), that it must not exceed a short paragraph in length, or that it must address certain elements. A mission statement should ideally suit each school and be a positive, succinct raison d'être. It shouldn't be expected to serve every purpose – the public relations brochure, the case for a capital campaign, the accreditation study– in one format.

The mission statement in many schools is enveloped in layers of protocol and is, rightfully, the property not just of the planning team. However, the planning process is a good vehicle for taking a fresh look at the mission statement to decide if it will stand up to the directions inherent in the emerging goals and the transcending ideas of the shared vision. If not, it is worth proposing that it be revamped by the faculty, administration, and any other constituents who wish to be involved, for adoption by the board.

Preliminary Priorities
With the rough draft of the policy goal sections and recommendations regarding the mission and educational philosophy statements in place, the planning team has completed almost all the work to be done in the workshop setting. Each of the policy goals will have a number of suggestions for implementation, perhaps as many as a dozen or more for some of the goals. (Please see the Germantown Academy Strategic Plan, in Appendix B.) It remains for the team to indicate the real strategic priorities, those half dozen or so critical components of the plan, particularly those that the team thinks must be addressed in the next year or two. Many of the implementation suggestions will in reality be business as usual; designating strategic priorities gives direction to the implementation program to be developed – starting points for specific action. Establishing strategic priorities also indicates where the school's energies must be focused, the themes and targets for board and administrative goals. Examples of strategic priorities are in some cases financial, in others curricular, in others directed towards student recruitment and retention or to faculty compensation and professional development.

I am indebted to David Bork, a planning and management consultant for family-owned businesses and my colleague for a large project, for showing me a simple, graphic way to allow a planning team to indicate relative priorities among implementation suggestions. That is to give each team member a strip of six or seven brightly colored gummed dot stickers and ask each person to place the dots next to those items on the newsprint sheets that he or she considers to be the six or seven implementation suggestions of greatest strategic priority. In a few minutes, the priorities on the newsprint sheets appear in a logical pattern that has evolved from all of the work of the process to this point, without additional rhetorical discussion.

The priorities recommended by the team, like all of the elements of the plan, will be subject to additional scrutiny, research, and development by others. However, the designation of even preliminary priorities will help people realize that the tasks are not overwhelming, help manage expectations of what is realistic in the short term, and give the administration and board significant help in designing the implementation program.

Oak Hall School, a 15-year-old elementary school in Ardmore, Oklahoma, engaged in the planning process several years after affiliating with the Episcopal Diocese of Oklahoma, improving and stabilizing what had been a bleak financial picture. Following years of near-disastrous leadership, a group of dedicated individuals had kept the school alive and it was again flourishing under new leadership. The classrooms in the Episcopal church, in an adjacent building leased from another church, and in a small house blocks away were bursting at the seams with students in the current program. At the end of an intensive, energy-charged planning workshop in which the planning team took stock of the school's current position and envisioned what they wanted the school to become, the red dots on the newsprint sheets showed the following to be the strategic priorities among the 74 implementation suggestions:

- Develop a master plan for the campus and its facilities.
- Initiate a fundraising plan for a building campaign.
- Pay competitive salaries.
- Maintain a low student-teacher ratio (a substantial competitive advantage locally).
- Seek accreditation with ISAS.

Each of these priority items with interlocking implications is a significant challenge for Oak Hall. The focus is clear and the school leadership is beginning to lay out exactly how to proceed with each, the sequencing of necessary action, and expected results to share within the extended school community.

Assignments
In the concluding session of the workshop, assignments should be made for the typing of the newsprint sheets, and members should be appointed to a drafting team to edit the rough draft emanating from the workshop. Also, who will communicate what to whom about the workshop content, and when a draft will be mailed to workshop participants should be agreed upon, along with a date for an editing meeting.

Strategic Thinking

The drafting team is most efficient when relatively small. Five to seven representatives of the planning team, including the school head and chair or co-chairs of the planning workshop, is about right. Whether the school head chooses to write a fist draft for the group to edit or shares that role with others, he or she must be integrally involved with writing the draft. The head has the best overview of school operations and will be the most closely involved with the implementation programming.

This is an example of a workshop agenda that corresponds with the process calendar found on page 20:

Sample Strategic Planning Workshop
Suggested Agenda for Review and Discussion

Day 1

6:00   Reception and dinner

7:00   Convene
       Introductions
       Planning process orientation
       Review of workshop agenda and objectives
       Discussion of background information

9:00   Adjourn

Day 2

8:00   Coffee

8:30   Convene
       Brainstorm external issues that may impact the school
       Brainstorm internal topics/issues to consider in planning for the future

10:00 *Break*

10:15 *Assign individual scenarios*

11:15 *Form discussion groups, review tasks; present and discuss individual scenarios*

(12:30 *Working lunch)*
Discussion groups work independently to develop consensus
Breaks as needed
Write elements of group scenarios on newsprint

5:30 *Break for reception/supper*

7:00 *Discussion groups present scenarios to full group*

9:00 *Adjourn*

Day 3

8:00 *Coffee*

8:30 *Convene*
Review process, day's agenda and objectives
The development of the planning report
Examples

8:45 *Compare group scenarios and begin drafting policy goals, rationales, and suggestions for implementation*

11:00 *Policy goal presentation and editing*

(12:00 *Working lunch)*
Complete policy goal work

1:30 *Appraisal of mission statement*
Strategic priorities
Communication with the school community
Next steps and assignments
Planning process calendar
Drafting the plan
Group editing meeting
Developing the implementation plan
Wrap-up

3:30 *Adjourn*

The following examples illustrate the workshop agendas I designed for the Grace School process, the outline of which is found on page 22.

Grace Church School
Strategic Planning Workshop I
November 14-15, 1991
Agenda

Thursday, November 14

3:30 *Refreshments*

4:00 *Convene*
Introduction
Process orientation
Background information
Appraisal of '84 plan

5:30 *Brainstorming external factors that may affect GCS in the future*

6:15 *Supper*

7:15 Brainstorming school topics and issues to consider in planning for the future
Wrap-up

9:00 Adjourn

Friday, November 15

8:00 Coffee

8:30 Convene

8:35 Individual scenarios

9:30 Assignment to discussion groups; tasks to be completed
Discussion groups work on own; breaks as needed

(12:00 Working lunch)

1:30 Discussion groups report
Clarification
Compare/contrast reports

3:00 Break

3:10 Complete tasks
Establish task forces, schedule, and meeting dates
Next steps
Wrap-up

4:00 Adjourn

Grace Church School
Strategic Planning Workshop II
January 25, 1992
Agenda

- 8:30   *Coffee*
- 9:00   *Convene*
  Discussion groups present reports: goals, rationale statements, and suggestions for implementation
- 10:00   *Break*
- 10:45   *Full group edits each section*
  Discussion/consensus
- (12:00   *Working lunch)*
- 12:45   *Complete editing*
- 2:45   *Break*
- 3:00   *Appraise mission statement*
  Strategic priorities
  Discuss: the development of the next draft;
      the presentation to the board
  Next steps and assignments
  Wrap-up
- 4:00   *Adjourn*

Chapter Four
Drafting the Strategic Plan

In writing a draft of the strategic plan from the results of the workshop (or workshops), the drafting team will want to use as much of the wording as possible directly from the typescript of the newsprint sheets; those sheets represent the synthesis of the small group scenarios into policy goal sections. The writers' task is to make critical revisions, however: to make the structure of the sections parallel; to add important points that may have been overlooked in the crush of time; and to draft from the raw material a concise document that represents the spirit of the workshop, yet is easy to read and understand for someone who was not a part of creating it.

The final written plan should be relatively short, straightforward, and focused on strategic issues and priorities. (Please see The Germantown Academy Plan in Appendix B.) The key to writing goal statements is to remember their umbrella function, but not to make them so broad that they become meaningless. I would emphasize again at this juncture that the suggestions for implementation that follow each goal represent an initial list for exploration; some may ultimately be found to be without merit, impossibly costly, or ideas whose time, for whatever reason, has not yet come. The suggestions for implementation form, in effect, a menu for those who will be charged with the actual responsibility for developing them further. They also represent the starting point for designing the implementation program to commit the school to action. They also make clear the implications of accepting the goals as valid within the strategic plan. To paraphrase Peter Drucker, even the best of intentions eventually degenerate into hard work. That sentiment describes succinctly the difference between goal statements and suggestions for implementation.

Politics, not surprisingly, can play a role in writing a draft that will be presented to the board and eventually throughout the school community. Good judgment will come into play in diplomatically rewriting what may appear bald in print. For instance, if there are delicate governance issues at stake, or confidential real estate negotiations involved, the way in which they are described in the plan could be critical to a successful outcome. Some items will be superfluous or poorly written, some will appear in more than one place, others may be factually incorrect or already underway. These kind of elements need to be altered, corrected, or deleted. This is not an unlimited license for the drafting team to go off on tangents of its own, since they are responsible for submitting the draft to the planning team for editing before it goes any further.

There may be some intriguing ideas that came up during the workshop but didn't make it through the winnowing process. Some schools have chosen to append these under a heading of "Interesting ideas to revisit later," or something similar. Other ideas may be considered by everyone

[margin note: Disposition of different kinds of items that arise]

to be good ones that could be implemented at little or no cost and should be by next week. Such ideas are not properly part of a strategic plan but can simply be passed along to the right person to take appropriate action.

Other components may be of such immediate strategic importance that action on them cannot be delayed until the plan has been formally adopted. Those components must be addressed at the right level in a timely manner. Examples of situations where quick action might be needed are: opportunities to acquire real estate; student recruitment or retention; or acting to create board diversity before a nominating process is so far along that a year would be lost awaiting approval of a complete document.

Ordering Priorities

During the workshop the implementation suggestions may have been divided into short, mid and long-term, or listed in a logical sequence or priority order. If not, the drafting team will want to so order them.

There is no assumption during the process that participants will agree on future directions, although general consensus tends to be the rule rather than the exception. That comes as a surprise to many who suspect that consensus does not exist. In cases where there is significant difference of opinion, a planning team has the option of proposing two opposing goals or a goal that directs resolution of the issue at hand.

In the late '70s, Holland Hall School, a PK-12 coeducational day school in Tulsa, operated on two separate campuses. Numerous facility issues that impinged on the program, including the image of the school in the community, maintenance, repair and replacement on the aging campus, and the disparity in quality between the two emerged as issues during a round of planning. The planning team was fairly evenly split as to whether the school should upgrade the older campus and maintain both physical and emotional ties to its original neighborhood or move the middle school from the old campus to the larger one in the southeast part of town where the primary and upper schools had been built. As part of the written plan, the team proposed that the board designate the necessary resources to appraise the property, retain architectural services to develop options (including costs), consult members of the school community, and amass all the data on which a realistic, strategic decision could be based. In time, the plan would be updated to reflect the results.

[margin note: real estate/master plan issues.]

There may be ambiguities in a draft plan from section to section that can only be resolved by further research or consulting with faculty and administrative staff who may not have been at the planning workshop. Brookwood School, an elementary school in the North Shore area outside Boston, had just completed some major capital improvements before beginning a new planning cycle in 1985. In one part of their newly created plan, it seemed clear that there would be no more such improvements during the span of the new implementation program. However, when the faculty began to study the recommendations for the program goals in depth, the realization that additional facilities were critical to meet proposed educational standards prompted school leadership to realign the plan and the implementation program.

The point is that the report of *recommendations* from the planning team cannot possibly address every eventuality. That is why there are two outcomes from this planning process: the recommendations of the goal framework representing the overall strategy, and the implementation program directing action. It is not the role of the members of the planning team to undertake the research and development of all the recommendations; their responsibility is to define the strategic goals that will direct and define the implementation program once the goals have been approved by the board.

The report being prepared for the board is an in-house working draft, not a public relations piece or the case statement for fundraising, although both may eventually be derived from it. Before presenting the working draft to the board, the planning team will be asked to reconvene for a final session, or two if the time is needed, to edit the draft and ensure that it is true to the work that preceded it, make any revisions, and plan for the board presentation. This is a vital aspect of keeping the sense of ownership of the plan alive, as well as an important procedural step. Without bringing the whole planning team together it is hard for a drafting team to know what revisions are acceptable if only written comments are solicited.

A checklist of sections in the draft includes:

- a brief description of the planning process
- an annotated list of planning team members
- any assumptions on which the plan is based
- a concisely stated vision of the school (many schools feel that the plan itself expresses this)
- the mission and philosophy statements
- the policy goals, each with a rationale and suggestions for implementation
- the strategic priorities
- a conclusion explaining the next steps in the process

During the drafting process it may be advisable to provide for a courtesy review by individuals who are important to the future of the school and who have not participated in the process thus far. The reviewer could be a major donor, a past board president, the rector of the parish or head of the vestry in a church-related school, or a key faculty member or administrator. Observing the "doctrine of no surprises" is important, particularly with individuals who may be outside the usual communication channels.

Presenting the Draft to the Board

Each school's culture will dictate in part the mode of transmission and presentation of the draft plan to the board. The report from the planning committee may be mailed in advance as custom dictates, or the decision may be to have all board members hear the report together. In either case, the meeting in which the report of the planning team is formally considered should be something of an event. (If most of the board members have participated in the process, the question may be moot.) Some schools choose to call a meeting at which the draft strategic plan will be the sole agenda item. Many schools invite members of the planning team who are not members of the board to be in attendance for the presentation and to participate in discussion. The challenge is to impart to the board some of the sense of excitement, enthusiasm, and commitment that inevitably has grown among members of the planning team and to focus the board's attention on the strategic goals and subsequent decisions that will be required. While the board will be asked to approve the mission and goals, recognizing the suggestions for implementation for what they represent, the planning team will want the board to understand clearly the import of those suggestions. After all the time and energy that has brought the planning process to the board level, one of the most deflating circumstances is a routine thanks and rapid move to the next committee report. Give thought to structuring a presentation that encourages questions, discussion, and perhaps even some editing by the board. <u>In other words, create the dynamics to engender some sense of ownership, not mere acceptance, by the board.</u>

The board will need to understand clearly that the draft plan precedes a specific implementation program. They need to know who is responsible, and what the timeline is for completion. Approval of the mission and goal framework provides the impetus for developing the implementation program– which will in turn be brought back for additional discussion and decisions as appropriate.

Ongoing Communication
Continuing communication is a vital part of the process, particularly in preparing a climate for change. The Germantown Academy approach is a good example of effective communication with parents. The school advised parents of the process before it was begun and actively solicited advance comments and suggestions. GA continued the communication schedule after board approval of the plan by mailing a letter, a copy of the plan, and a form seeking comments. (Please see the Germantown Academy documents in Appendix B.)

Hawaii's Punahou School, NAIS's largest member school with some 3700 students in PK-12, carefully and thoughtfully structured school communications throughout their planning process. The leadership began that communication by presenting several lectures pertinent to future planning during the course of Punahou's sesquicentennial year celebrations. During the next academic year, before a planning workshop, a series of meetings were scheduled in which all faculty, administrators, parents, members of the Alumni Association boards, and student leaders were invited to participate. The meetings were facilitated by members of the school community who had attended a training session preparation. Facilitators each led a group of fewer than 15 people through an agenda designed to elicit ideas not only about the future, but also about what people valued most about Punahou in the present. The resulting volumes of information were compiled for the planning group and also summarized and made available to those who had attended meetings. Articles were written for the various constituent newsletters to keep everyone informed about progress and results throughout the active planning year.

These are examples of communication that not only informs people, but also invites participation and helps to manage expectations, positive and negative. I have found that it is a useful rule of thumb not to ask for what isn't wanted and can't be used. Therefore, if there is no *mechanism* for feedback, nor the intention to use it, asking for it only builds frustration.

The timing of seeking feedback should be judged carefully. During planning meetings for The Columbus Academy, at the time an elementary and secondary school for boys, it became clear that the future vision included some version of coeducation. Once school leadership had examined the ramifications, a questionnaire was sent to members of the Columbus Academy community to determine the desire for and reactions to several different configurations of coeducation. Both consulting those who would be affected and the information that was gathered in the process proved invaluable in making strategic decisions.

Chapter Five
The Implementation Program

The report to the board represents a plausible future and a broad strategy for a school. The board's acceptance represents the approval to go ahead and develop the implementation program based on the strategic thinking. The foundation for implementing the plan has been laid from the very beginning of the process. Strategic thinking deals with where you want to be at a point in the future; implementation deals with how you will get there – beginning today.

The head of school is the chief architect responsible for designing the implementation program. The head will want to consult with members of the administrative team, faculty, board, leaders of the parent and alumni/ae associations, and student body, according to his or her personal style. The charge is to create a specific sequential implementation program containing:

- the assignment of measurable actions to individuals (by name, by title, committee name, special task force designation)
- timelines for completion of each action item
- financial resources needed

- where final authority for approval lies
- when the action should be appraised
- a column for appraisal and progress notes

Priorities for implementation may in some cases be clear from the planning team report; in others priority is dependent on further work and research during the implementation phase. Divide actions to be assigned into those that will be initiated in the next year and then in succeeding years; the result may be a three-year or a five-year operating plan.

It is important to note is that there is a tendency to try to schedule what should realistically take five years into one, and to commit at least 200 percent of administrators' time. Such tendencies become apparent in filling out an implementation matrix (see Appendices). Remember that a school cannot carry out the program of the future with only current resources in terms of personnel configurations or (usually) within current financial resources. An implementation program must recognize reality and attempt to project future needs in light of the goals. They may not all be realizable, or realistic in the short term. The discipline in the design of the implementation program is to delineate realistic, measurable objectives, understanding that many will in turn prefigure the next generation of actions. Those elements that are known to be truly long-term should not be deleted from the implementation program, but listed as actions to be explored in five years or more.

Who Takes Part?
One way to create an implementation program is for the school head to work with designated individuals. Another model is exemplified by the Kent Denver School, a coeducational day school for students from the 6th through the 12th grade.

The planning tradition at Kent Denver is one of broad participation. When the school installed a new head, one of his objectives was to update the strategic plan. With the recommendations of the planning team and board approval in place, the goal sections were assigned to eight standing and special committees for discussion. Each was charged with engaging in initial research to formulate both priorities and the implementation program for its assigned goals. The committees comprised administrators, faculty members, board members, parents, alumni/ae, and, in some instances, outside professional advisors. Many of the committees employed ad hoc subcommittees to ensure adequate consideration of each implementation action. Hundreds of hours of work were summarized into key recommendations which, taken together, make up the implementation program. The section on program, for example, reads as follows. It, like all other examples in this book, is printed here with the school's permission.

Program

Kent Denver will continue to prepare young men and women for college and beyond through a study of the liberal arts. Within the program there will be emphasis on problem solving, critical thinking, creative expression, effective communication, team building and physical fitness, community service and global awareness.

Rationale

Our society is changing rapidly. Kent Denver students will live in a more interdependent world. They will need to be articulate and technically competent; they will need a system of values and a breadth of education that will enable them to live responsibly in a diverse world.

Suggested Implementation Actions

Short Term (1-2 years)
- Create a sense of community, school spirit and place for students. (Board, administration, faculty)
- Maintain the strength of the school's language program and enhance whenever possible. (Administration, faculty)
- Examine the scope and structure of the performing arts program with the purpose of attaining balance and excellence in several areas. (Administration, faculty)
- Maintain the strength of the athletic programs. (Administration, faculty)
- Strengthen the community service program. (Administration, faculty)
- Consider a 9th/10th (or 11th) grade special program that might have multicultural, interdisciplinary, international, and service components. (Faculty, administration)
- Re-examine the computer literacy requirement for students on an annual basis. (Faculty)
- Monitor learning technology and its potential for assisting teachers and enhancing the learning process. (Administration, faculty)
- Strengthen the school's physical education program by considering such options as Outward Bound, outdoor education, etc., while not diluting the current athletic program. (Administration, faculty)
- Maintain class sizes of 15 to 20 students. (Administration)

- Increase sensitivity to multiculturalism throughout the curriculum. (Administration, faculty)
- Develop outreach programs through business alliances, cooperative programs with universities, a scholar-in residence program, a visiting lecture program that brings interesting visitors on the campus for a period of time, and faculty and student exchanges. (Administration, faculty)
- Consider lengthening the school year. (Administration, faculty)
- Consider a before- and after-school program to assist families with one parent or with both parents working. (Board, administration)

Long Term (3-5 years)
- Consider a K-5th grade program for Kent Denver School. (Board, administration)

. . . .

Resource Allocation

Planning is linked to resource allocation not at its inception but in the implementation programming. Kent Denver examples are the program section of the report from the committee charged with designing the actual implementation, and the detailed financial projection. Both documents follow:

The Implementation Program

Committee on Program

The challenge for the program is to chart new directions while remaining true to the liberal arts and college preparatory tradition.

In the '90s, technology poses obvious challenges to all schools. Computer, video, cable, and other electronic data sources provide new learning opportunities, but they can be expensive and cumbersome. Kent Denver is experimenting with this new technology and will encourage all faculty to become more comfortable with these developments before the end of 1994.

An increasingly global economy coupled with growing diversity in the population of the United States dictates changes in curriculum and in the school community. Multicultural perspectives are as important as a student body and staff that mirror current demography. Hiring of teachers of color has not kept pace with our progress in the other areas and must be a special concern in the years ahead.

New direction for the formal program for 9th and 10th graders encourages making learning more vital and engaging. Experimental learning, interdisciplinary work, and multicultural emphasis have great potential for these underclassmen. Teachers and advisors at these levels are pursuing an array of possibilities that interest them.

The Alumni Association is collaborating with the school to develop a program that will bring distinguished visitors to campus to spend time with students and offer lectures to the wider community.

We have considered the addition of an elementary division (K-5) but decided to put that aside for the time being.

Creating a school that functions as a community despite long commutes and disparate neighborhoods is a challenge that can be met as we find more ways to embrace differences and to express our shared purposes.

Key Recommendations
1. Learning Technology
   a) Professional advancement for all faculty prior to the academic year 1994-1995 in order to implement appropriate technology in classes of all teachers.
   b) Increased hardware and software for classroom use.
   c) Replacement of antiquated language laboratory with state-of-the-art equipment.
2. All faculty and staff searches include a person of color as finalist. Special efforts are being taken to increase minority applicant pool.
3. Faculty continues to modify curriculum for 9th and 10th graders so that basic skills and intellectual enthusiasm are enhanced.
4. A committee involving the Alumni Association and the school staff creates a program to bring distinguished guests to campus.
5. School leadership continues to focus on building a strong community.
6. The school retains its existing 6-12 grade structure.

Funding Requirements

1. Technology

a) Professional development	$ 10,000	*(2 years)*
b) Software	25,000	*(5 years)*
c) Classroom computers	20,000	
d) Replace language laboratory	50,000	
Sub-total	**105,000**	

2. 9th and 10th Grade Program $ 10,000 *(per year)*
3. Visiting Lecturers   2,000 *(per year)*

Total   **$117,000**

. . . .

The Kent Denver example shows that as the implementation program is developed and as research is reported, school leadership is in a position to make strategic decisions consistent with the mission. It is not unusual for action items in a plan to exceed a school's resources. It is not until the extent is known that options and alternatives can be considered and real, schoolwide priorities established. Is it more important, if a choice must be made, to build additional facilities or to increase faculty compensation. The decision cannot be made in a vacuum.

Multi-year financial planning and forecasting are at the core of an effective implementation program. Kent Denver, as a concluding piece of the evolving process described above, made this report to the board of trustees, in which actions and recommendations were separated into two parts – those that required little or no funding and those that would require capital funding.

Shaping Strategy

Kent Denver School
Englewood, Colorado

May 1, 1992

Strategic Planning Report

To: Kent Denver Board of Trustees
From: The Executive Committee and School Administration
Re: Strategic Planning Recommendations

The Executive Committee and school administration have reviewed the long-range planning reports and recommendations. The following recommendations are made to the Board of Trustees for their discussion, approval or amendment.

I.   We recommend that the Board of Trustees endorse those actions and recommendations that require minimal or no funding. See list of actions on page 4.

II. We recommend that the Board of Trustees endorse the capital needs as presented below. Approval does not imply a decision to move forward and raise funds. It signals the board's agreement that these capital projects are needed and would be funded if we had the resources.

The Implementation Program

A. *Endowment*

1. Faculty and staff salaries: $3,900,000
   (or $215,000 in increased operating funds)

2. Professional development: $ 460,000
   (or $25,000 more in operating funds)

3. Financial aid: $1,000,000
   (If endowment were raised
   it would relieve $55,000 in
   operating budget

4. Lecturer fund: $ 50,000
   (or $3,000 more in operating funds)

5. Student support fund: $ 182,000
   (or $10,000 more in operating funds)

   Total $5,592,000

good method to present endowment along w/ annual funding as an alternative

75

B. *Physical Plant Improvements*

1. Traffic plan:	$	125,000*
2. Language lab:	$	50,000 – $70,000**
3. Varsity baseball field:	$	85,000
4. Weight room: (near upper school gym)	$	80,000***
5. Two tennis courts:	$	62,000
6. New entrance to upper school/store: (not defined)		
7. Middle school plaza:	$	50,000
Total		**$ 352,000**
Grand Total		**$5,944,000**

*   No reliable estimate yet
** Preliminary research only
*** Assumes new construction

C. *Other Projects Listed by Annual Budgets*

After some thought it seemed logical to assign the following projects to the operating budget because of their nature, the timing of need, or the magnitude of need. Specifically, we would propose that the following budgets be used:

1. New floor in field house:	$43,000
2. Computer training for teachers:	$10,000
3. Computers:	$20,000
4. Professional photography for admissions:	$ 4,000
5. Media/PR support:	$ 2,000 - 4,000*
6. 9th & 10th grade program:	$ 5,000 - 20,000*
Total	**$84,000 - 108,000**

* Not fully defined

III. **Notes**
A. *6th Grade Expansion*

The long-range plan does not include current deliberations about expanding from two to three 6th grade sections (50 to 75 students). Should expansion be seen as financially feasible, it is assumed that, with the possible exception of (Option 3.) below, the physical plant modifications would be covered by increased revenue.

1. Physical plant modification costs
   a) Temporary facilities *$12,000*
   b) Permanent facilities

   Option 1. Renovate business/development offices into classroom; move offices to the residence hall   Cost: *$130,000*

   Option 2. Add new wing to middle school building; leave offices alone
   Cost: *$150,000*

   Option 3. Renovate business/development offices into classroom; move offices to renovated administrative area in upper school   Cost: *$265,000*

2. Next steps

The Finance Committee and administration are studying projection costs, revenues, and program modifications. The timetable for the decision is as follows:

a) Consult the Board of Trustees in June, 1992 about financial feasibility

b) Study program modifications, outline marketing plan and physical plant options in the summer

c) September or October, 1992, make recommendations to the Board of Trustees

B. *Water Distribution System*

This long-range plan also does not include the upgrading of the campus water distribution system. The Board will ultimately have to determine whether it funds the project (estimated now at approximately $500,000) through funds received earlier from the sale of water rights, or through future fundraising, or a combination of the two sources. A recommendation on the project will be presented by June, 1992.

Strategic Planning Projects

Implementation Actions and Recommendations Requiring Minimal or No Funding

I. Committee on Program

   A. *Implementation Action Plans Completed*
   1. Examine the scope and structure of the fine arts program.
   2. If possible, all faculty and staff searches will include a person of color as a finalist.
   3. Create a sense of community, school spirit and place for students.
   4. Consider a K-5th grade program. Recommendation: Retain existing 6-12 grade structure.

   B. *Implementation Actions Ongoing*
   1. Develop outreach programs.
      - business alliances
      - cooperative programs with universities
      - scholar-in-residence program
      - faculty and student exchanges
   2. Increase sensitivity to multiculturalism throughout the curriculum.

   C. *Implementation Actions Deferred or Deleted*
   1. Strengthen the physical education program while not diluting the current athletic programs.

II. Alumni Association Board

A. *Implementation Action Plans Completed*
None

B. *Implementation Actions Ongoing*
1. Focus attention on Kent Denver graduates.
2. Publish an alumni directory.
   Some funding required.
3. Increase alumni involvement with the school.

C. *Implementation Actions Deferred or Deleted*
None

D. *Implementation Actions Added*
1. Review the possibility of sharing the use of school facilities and programs with the alumni.
2. Organize regional alumni reunions.

III. Parents Association Board

A. *Implementation Action Plans Completed*
1. Set up *accounting procedures* in accordance with the school's system.
2. Redesign *parent* volunteer forms.
3. Maintain the Parent Information Network Drug and Alcohol Committee.

B. *Implementation Actions Ongoing*
1. Work to create a greater sense of community.

C. *Implementation Actions Deferred or Deleted*
1. Consider a separate handbook for parents.

IV. **Buildings and Grounds Committee**
   A. *Implementation Action Plans Completed*
      1. Study the utilization of facilities as a means of determining the school's enrollment potential.
      2. Consider the need for a larger upper school meeting space.
      Recommendation: Experiment with using the gymnasium.
   B. *Implementation Actions Ongoing*
      None
   C. *Implementation Actions Deferred*
      1. Determine the core campus as it relates to the land required for current and future programs.

V. **Finance Committee**
   A. *Implementation Action Plans Completed*
      1. Determine the feasibility of a program of paid leaves.
      (Determined to be not feasible at this time.)
      2. Review the policy for tuition remission for faculty children. (Recommended no changes to the policy.)
   B. *Implementation Actions Ongoing*
      1. Develop a comprehensive financial plan. A five-year plan will be completed by June, 1992.
   C. *Implementation Actions Deferred or Deleted*
      None

VI. Development Committee

A. *Implementation Action Plans Completed*
   1. Complete the fundraising for the renovation of El Pomar Hall.

B. *Implementation Actions Ongoing*
   1. Increase the support of the annual fund.
   2. Establish a program of planned giving.
   3. Establish a schedule for the cultivation and solicitation of foundations and individuals.

C. *Implementation Actions Deferred or Deleted*
   None

D. *Implementation Actions Added*
   1. Continue the tradition of an annual parents' benefit.

E. *Implementation Actions Revised*
   1. The goal of increasing the annual fund to 10% of the operating budget within 3-5 years is unrealistic.

VII. Board of Trustees

A. *Implementation Action Plans Completed*
   1. Expand the orientation process for new trustees.
   2. Develop plans for identifying and cultivating candidates for the board.
   3. Refine the process of evaluating the headmaster.

B. *Implementation Actions Ongoing*
   1. Seek ethnic diversity among the members of the board.
   2. Consider ways to continue the involvement of former trustees.

C. *Implementation Actions Deferred or Deleted*
   None

VIII. **Marketing Committee**

A/B. *Implementation Action Plans Completed and Ongoing*
   1. Research the competition for students.
   2. Audit school publications.
   3. Develop a marketing plan.
   4. Establish and implement promotional strategies.
   5. Increase enrollment.
   6. Continue to attract a diverse student body.
   7. Review the scope of the financial aid program.
   8. Examine the feasibility of a more comprehensive transportation system.
   9. Consider the need for before-and-after school programs.
   10. Continue efforts to reduce student attrition.

C. *Implementation Actions Deferred or Deleted*
   1. Articulate the unique nature of the school in publications.
   2. Consider new pricing strategies.
      Deferred to the Finance Committee.
   3. Consider the viability of merit scholarships.

Spreadsheet Forecasting

Another efficacious approach to financial planning is spreadsheet forecasting. Software programs that can be employed for this purpose are readily available commercially. The purpose is to project what the financial picture might be under certain circumstances and based on various assumptions. For example, in order to raise salaries a certain percentage and increase the financial aid budget, factoring in a specified inflation rate for all other expense items, what would tuition and annual giving levels have to be over a period of years? Are the answers acceptable? Realistic? Palatable? If not, then what alternatives exist?

The administration of Greensboro Day School, North Carolina, a coeducational day school for approximately 750 students, developed the projection model on the following pages for its board to use in analyzing the financial issues inherent in the plan they had approved in the middle '80s.

Shaping Strategy

Greensboro Day School Forecast Model August 1, 1990

Year Type	87–88 Actual	88–89 Actual	89–90 Budget	90–91 Projected	91–92 Projected	92–93 Projected	93–94 Projected	94–95 Projected
Assumptions								
Enrollment								
Kindergarten	57	53	55	55	55	56	57	57
Grades 1–6	323	346	341	342	340	340	340	340
Grades 7–12	306	320	334	340	354	368	370	376
Total	686	719	730	737	749	764	767	773
Inflation Assumption	4.5	4.5	5.5	5	5	5	5	5
Interest Rate Assumption	8.75	10	10.5	10	9.5	9.5	9.5	9.5
ROR – Cash −1	6.75	9	9.5	9	8.5	8.5	8.5	8.5
ROR – Endowment −1	6.75	9	9.5	9	8.5	8.5	8.5	8.5
Tuition Change	8.3	7.9	9.3	8.9	9.4	9.2	8.6	7.25
Kindergarten	2,300	2,600	3,000	3,267	3,594	3,924	4,262	4,571
Grades 1–6	4,215	4,550	4,975	5,418	5,962	6,511	7,071	7,583
Grades 7–12	4,675	5,050	5,550	6,044	6,646	7,257	7,882	8,453
Fees Change	0	4.5	5.5	5	5	5	5	5
Salary Change 2.5	4	7	7.5	7.5	7.5	7.5	7.5	7.5
Mean Salary	22,631	24,215	25,597	27,517	28,872	31,038	33,366	35,868
New Program Staffing		1.08	2.98	3.00	1.22	0.97	0.83	0.7
Faculty FTE	63.24	64.32	68.03	70.30	72.09	74.50	75.62	76.92
Student/Faculty Ratio	10.85	11.18	10.73	10.48	10.39	10.25	10.14	10.05

The Implementation Program

Greensboro Day School Forecast Model — August 1, 1990

Year Type		87–88 Actual	88–89 Actual	89–90 Budget	90–91 Projected	91–92 Projected	92–93 Projected	93–94 Projected	94–95 Projected
Current Year Operating Budget									
Tuition		2,971,367	3,346,309	3,715,175	4,087,604	4,577,542	5,104,205	5,563,192	6,017,242
Fees		281,671	313,703	327,769	347,465	367,700	393,817	415,131	439,298
Annual Giving	0.1	115,551	148,125	140,000	154,000	178,200	196,020	215,622	237,184
Endowment		16,878	22,787	16,700	17,816	16,433	17,127	17,850	18,603
Other	0.06	218,195	267,537	230,000	315,181	300,673	334,683	364,713	394,052
Total Revenues		3,603,662	4,098,461	4,429,644	4,922,066	5,440,549	6,045,852	6,576,508	7,106,379
Salaries	0.06	2,098,892	2,325,895	2,596,794	2,937,266	3,161,148	3,506,807	3,824,099	4,178,046
Benefits	0.185	362,378	433,810	495,112	499,335	619,812	683,759	742,458	807,939
Instructional	ROI	179,606	208,144	204,729	214,965	246,580	256,909	267,755	279,142
Transportation	ROI	42,391	30,153	36,150	37,958	37,958	39,855	41,848	43,941
Maintenance	ROI	199,258	218,862	227,185	238,544	277,987	341,507	358,582	376,512
Gen Admin.	ROI	186,752	225,563	222,510	233,636	252,373	262,992	274,141	285,848
Athletics	ROI	48,121	59,870	62,330	65,447	74,839	78,581	82,510	86,635
Financial Aid	0	175,795	186,730	205,246	223,513	276,146	301,552	327,485	351,228
Faculty Scholar.	0	108,780	132,350	166,675	188,797	208,140	231,069	251,861	271,724
Transfer to Debt		0	77,948	30,000	30,000	30,000	30,000	30,000	30,000
PPRRSM/Veh	0.015	50,000	55,500	76,000	73,831	77,000	85,000	98,648	106,596
Dev Exp/Transfer from CC				0	50,000	76,000	119,000	163,000	169,000
Other		89,636	141,876	107,766	127,562	101,988	107,087	112,441	118,063
Total Expense		3,541,609	4,096,701	4,430,497	4,920,854	5,439,970	6,044,118	6,574,828	7,104,673
Surplus (Loss)		62,053	1,760	(853)	1,212	579	1,734	1,679	1,706

Shaping Strategy

Greensboro Day School Forecast Model August 1, 1990

Year Type	87-88 Actual	88-89 Actual	89-90 Budget	90-91 Projected	91-92 Projected	92-93 Projected	93-94 Projected	94-95 Projected
Unexpected Plant Fund								
Debt	1,189,164	1,050,658	998,415	864,934	782,116	737,372	685,240
Items Decreasing Debt								
Gifts		(183,149)	(50,000)		(50,000)	0	0	0
From Campaign		0	0	0	0	0	0	0
From Operating		(77,948)	(30,000)	(30,000)	(30,000)	(30,000)	(30,000)	(30,000)
Income from Rentals		(29,342)	(32,116)	(35,327)	(22,000)	(24,200)	(26,620)	(29,282)
Receivables		(60,000)	(6,300)	(6,930)	(7,408)	(8,111)	(8,882)	(9,726)
Interest Earned		0	0	0	0	0	0	0
Membership Certificates		(121,950)	(115,000)	(115,000)	(125,000)	(125,000)	(125,000)	(125,000)
Items Increasing Debt								
Interest Expense		129,852	110,319	99,841	82,169	74,301	70,050	65,098
To/From Operating Budget		(1,760)	853	(1,212)	(579)	(1,734)	(1,679)	(1,706)
To Expanded Plant Fund		119,400	30,000	30,000	30,000	30,000	30,000	30,000
To Endowment Funds		0	0	0	0	0	0	0
Membership Redemptions		63,000	40,000	40,000	40,000	40,000	40,000	40,000
End Balance	1,189,164	1,027,267	998,415	929,787	782,116	737,372	685,240	624,625
Change		(161,897)	(52,243)	(68,628)	(82,818)	(44,745)	(52,131)	(60,616)
Endowment								
Beginning Balance	373,000	381,713	391,925	410,498	434,748	453,094	472,214	492,142
Increase	0	0	0	0	0	0	0	0
Income	27,043	32,446	35,273	34,892	34,780	36,248	37,777	39,371
Total	400,043	414,158	427,198	445,390	469,527	489,341	509,992	531,513
To Other Funds	18,330	15,000	16,700	17,816	16,433	17,127	17,850	18,603
Ending Balance	381,713	399,158	410,498	427,574	453,094	472,214	492,142	512,910
PPRRSM/Vehicle Replacement								
Beginning Balance	119,200	157,076	161,500	159,535	146,023	184,705	209,481	299,887
Additions	50,000	55,500	76,000	73,831	77,000	85,000	98,648	106,596
Earnings	8,642	8,624	14,535	13,560	11,682	14,776	16,759	23,991
Expense	20,766	59,700	92,500	81,500	50,000	75,000	25,000	0
Ending	157,076	161,500	159,535	165,426	184,705	209,481	299,887	430,474

Greensboro Day School Forecast Model August 1, 1990

Summary Forecast

Year Type	87–88 Actual	88–89 Actual	89–90 Budget	90–91 Projected	91–92 Projected	92–93 Projected	93–94 Projected	94–95 Projected
Summary Forecast								
Total Enrollment	686	719	730	737	749	764	767	773
Inflation Rate	4.5	4.5	5.5	5	5	5	5	5
Interest Rate	8.75	10	10.5	10	9.5	9.5	9.5	9.5
Tuition Change	8.30	7.90	9.30	8.90	9.40	9.20	8.60	7.25
Kindergarten	2,300	2,600	3,000	3,257	3,594	3,924	4,262	4,571
Grades 1–6	4,215	4,550	4,975	5,418	5,962	6,511	7,071	7,583
Grades 7–12	4,675	5,050	5,550	6,044	6,646	7,257	7,882	8,453
Salary Change	4.00	7.00	7.50	7.50	7.50	7.50	7.50	7.50
Mean Salary	22,631	24,215	25,597	27,517	28,872	31,038	33,366	35,868
Faculty FTE	63.24	64.32	68.03	70.30	72.09	74.50	75.62	76.92
Net Ratio	10.85	11.18	10.73	10.48	10.39	10.25	10.14	10.05
Net Profit (Loss)	62,053	1,760	(853)	1,212	579	1,734	1,679	1,706
Debt Balance	1,189,164	1,027,267	998,415	929,787	782,116	737,372	685,240	624,625
Endowment Balance	381,713	399,158	410,498	427,574	453,094	472,214	492,142	512,910
PPRRSM Balance	157,076	161,500	159,535	165,426	184,705	209,481	299,887	430,474
Non-Faculty Scholarship	175,795	186,730	205,246	223,513	276,146	301,552	327,485	351,228
Faculty Scholarship	108,780	132,350	166,675	188,797	208,140	231,069	251,861	271,724
Scholarship Equivalents	60.87	63.18	67.01	68.22	72.87	73.39	73.51	73.70
Scholarship % of Budget	8.04%	7.79%	8.39%	8.38%	8.90%	8.81%	8.81%	8.77%
Scholarship % of Enrollment	8.87%	8.79%	9.18%	9.26%	9.73%	9.61%	9.58%	9.53%
Annual Giving Total	115,551	148,125	140,000	154,000	178,200	196,020	215,622	237,184

Cautions here are that the Greensboro forecast is *not* a budget and that there is a definite distinction between annual budgeting and financial forecasting. The latter lets a school anticipate and plan for needs and demands in years to come and estimate answers to questions such as: What items in the strategic plan might be funded from operating income, special grants, or a capital campaign? How long might it take, ongoing needs considered, to raise faculty salaries to desired levels? What happens to the total the annual fund must raise if tuitions aren't raised for several years? Or, conversely, what must the school forego if tuitions (or giving, or earned income) are kept level? All answers to ponder in making strategic decisions.

Neil Cullen, Business Manager for Phillips Academy, a coeducational boarding and day school in Andover, Massachusetts, for 200 students from grade 9 through a postgraduate program, discussed cost containment measures at the school during a presentation at the NAIS Annual Conference in 1991. Cullen stated, "In a healthy and growing economy, wealthy and not-so-wealthy institutions alike spend according to their means and on the basis of optimistic revenue forecasts. Wealthy institutions simply spend at higher levels and therefore create more momentum. Endowment funds can help cushion the fall in the short term, but well-endowed schools must also adjust fairly quickly to a bleaker economic picture if they hope to sustain themselves."

In describing the financial picture at Andover, he explains that on concluding the school's second strategic plan in 1988, the thought was that the school could continue to achieve major objectives within a balanced budget. But the actual revenue and expense patterns reveal that they did not fully anticipate the increased demand for financial aid; that the objective of raising faculty compensation by 50% earlier than projected thus cost much more in benefits than expected; that tuition was raised at a more aggressive rate than forecast and could not continue at the current pace; that endowment income must grow even more to meet spending patterns; and, finally, that Andover had fallen short of funding annual plant renewal needs from operations. Seeing the figures, the school determined to check the problems.

What happened as a result? Cullen described a broadly participatory process initiated to focus on the challenges and to build a community consensus on how to balance the next year's budget. There were several key ingredients: a mandate by the board of trustees, a decision by the headmaster to make budget reduction the principal administrative business through the fall, participation by administrators and their subordinates schoolwide, and faculty involvement. Finally, Cullen said, "We based the reductions on the school priorities as specified in our long range plan. Having the plan proved invaluable since we did not have to debate which aspects of the school were more important than others."

Cullen provided an excellent insight into the problems of financial planning and of the results of a consistent appraisal of *actual* performance versus what is *projected*. Having achieved the objective of a balanced budget for the ensuing year, Cullen speaks to the future. "Reviewing our strategic plan will focus the community's attention on the importance of consciously seeking financial equilibrium [by maintaining] four basic financial conditions:

1. Current income equals or exceeds current expenses.
2. The growth of income equals or exceeds the growth of expenses.
3. The endowment spending level preserves the endowment's real purchasing power net of inflation.
4. Spending and/or creating reserves for renewal and replacement of the physical plant and for equipment is sufficient to preserve their useful life."

Andover's experience points out issues surrounding who makes decisions, the levels at which they are made, communications within the school community, and education of constituencies about decisions. Appraisal of the plan and the ensuing corrective action were consistent with the process used originally to conceive the plan.

Authority and Responsibility
All of the points in the implementation program will not necessarily require board approval. Those involving operations will be under the aegis of the head, including curricular initiatives (where the faculty has primacy), admissions activities, compensation and professional development, marketing, town-gown relations, student life, college counseling and other similar areas. The board will be primarily responsible for governance issues, finance, development, and any matters regarding school policy that normally entail board sanction. There are areas of mutual responsibility, such as funding facilities maintenance, large capital expenditures, determining compensation goals, and tuition positions, for example.

Each objective within the implementation program will have a different timeline, a different supporting cast, and a different locus of authority. (For examples, please see the implementation programs for St. Martin's Episcopal School and for Germantown Academy in the Appendices.)

Principles of Implementation
When designing a practical implementation program, observe the following principles:

- The points for action should be written beginning with verbs, and should be clear, specific and measurable.
- The points for action should be listed in order of priority or by time sequence, i.e. short-, mid-, long-term.
- Each action item will be assigned to an individual, a designated committee, or other identifiable entity.
- The period of time in which action is to be initiated and completed must be explicit.
- Financial resources necessary will be estimated.
- The locus of approval and authority will be determined.
- Responsibility and timing for regular appraisal will be indicated.

Perhaps most important, the implementation program should include ways to consult with appropriate people and portions of the school community as to future directions and decisions. Similarly, those individuals who will be involved in executing elements of the implementation program must also be involved in some way in making the plans they will be asked to put into practice. Finally, elements of the implementation program must be communicated throughout the school.

Chapter Six
Appraisal and Revitalization

Appraisal and reassessment ensure that leadership remains sensitive to variables. Strategic thinking is future oriented; strategic choices are in the present and their results must be monitored constantly. The Andover story directs attention to the need to frame a method for systematically monitoring and appraising the plan and the implementation program. That may be the responsibility of a school's standing planning committee, the executive committee of the board, or an ad hoc committee composed of members of the board, the administration, and the faculty. The purpose of appraisal is to monitor results, to decide whether corrections should be made, and to update the plan. Results of specific actions – including completed research – may then alter the implementation program.

Timing the Appraisal
The goals in the plan will probably not change significantly over a period of several years. They are, however, subject to reassessment particularly if affected by dislocating factors either externally or internally. The implementation program will be the principal focus for formal appraisal and read-

justment during the first several years after conceiving a new plan. In order to remain strategic, a plan must be constantly revised; it is a dynamic document, particularly in implementation.

Timing and flexibility are key components in implementing a plan. A case in point is that of Holland Hall School (see page 60). After the requisite research was done, school leadership decided to sell the older campus and raise money to build a new middle school on the larger campus. This part of the plan was implemented, happily, in about three years, just before the precipitous fall of the price of oil in 1982. Because it serves a community with an economy largely based on the petroleum industry, Holland Hall immediately reassessed its planning priorities and supporting resources to adjust to new economic realities. Although constrained from further capital expansion through the remainder of the last decade, the school was able to realize its dream of constructing a fine and performing arts facility in 1992, an integral program component of the original '70s plan.

Oversight Roles

The group charged with gathering information for an objective ongoing appraisal will be reporting primarily to the head of school and to the board. Questions asked by each should be related to their respective roles – the head's for operations and the board's for policy. According to the *NAIS Trustee Handbook*, institutional planning is an essential part of the board's oversight responsibilities. Therefore, a closer examination of the board's role in appraising and updating the plan is in order.

The Association of Governing Boards of Universities and Colleges has published two books that are useful in creating a systematic approach to appraising a plan. *Strategic Decision Making: Key Questions and Indicators for Trustees* lists questions appropriate for trustees to ask. *Strategic Analysis: Using Comparative Data to Understand Your Institution* analyzes how schools can use databases to assess performance against a number of indicators. The latter book makes the point that trustees cannot and moreover should not concern themselves with analyzing all available information or operating details. Rather they must concern themselves with those indicators that affect the strategic position of the school and with information that will support their strategic decision-making. In businesses, strategy seeks to define sustainable competitive advantages; in educational institutions, according to *Strategic Analysis*, "...strategy is finding the paradigms that promote institutional aims and mission."

A measure of overall performance that is clearly within the board's purview, and one on which many boards tend to focus almost to the exclusion of others, is financial performance and budget review. While boards must be adept in monitoring financial data, that cannot be their sole focus. Michael Goold, director of the Asbridge Strategic Management Centre in London, wrote an article in the Winter 1991 *Sloan Management Review* equating formal and informal implementation methods with what he calls "strategic control." Goold writes that "Budgetary control... stresses profit and other financial objectives such as cash flow, and concentrates mainly or exclusively on the coming twelve months. It does not cover nonfinancial objectives that may be important to achieving secure profitability and competitive strength; it pays no attention to long-term goals and objectives. Strategic control is concerned with the successful implementation of strategic plans, just as budgetary control focuses on the achievement of budget targets... . Thus, the strategic control process is concerned not only with feedback... on results achieved, but also with rapid adjustment to strategies that are encountering problems."

There is a need for consistent and appropriate data for trustees to use to fulfill their oversight responsibility. Such data also serve to alert school leadership to adjustments that may be needed in either the plan or the implementation program.

Gathering some of this information is quite straightforward – essentially involving constant updating of the data gathered at the beginning of the planning cycle. Monitoring progress in faculty compensation toward stated goals (which tend to be moving targets), examining trends in student recruitment and retention, and analyzing changes in student-faculty ratios or class size, for example, can be fairly easily accomplished through regular and consistent reporting of the data.

On the other hand, it is much more difficult to assess the results of an emphasis on diversity and multicultural issues, a change in the school ethos or moral climate, or the progress toward implementing program elements. Faculty, student, and parent feedback through questionnaires and survey methods can yield this more subjective kind of information.

Working together, the board (perhaps through the strategic planning committee) and administrative team can develop lists of indicators and outcomes that correspond to strategic initiatives and priorities appropriate for board review in addition to the "bottom line."

Getting to Appraisal

The appraisal mechanism outlined within an individual school should be based on the construction of the implementation program itself. (Please see the implementation programs for St. Martin's Episcopal School and Germantown Academy in Appendix B.) An ad hoc or a standing committee made up of members of the administration, faculty, trustees, and others according to a school's needs is usually charged with overseeing progress toward implementation. The school head is a prime mover in the implementation process, since so many of the actions are operational in nature; so also must the head take a leadership role in the implementation phase.

Simply stated, for each item that is listed to implement a given goal, the committee responsible for overseeing appraisal should ask for a progress report from those designated to carry out the action. Was action initiated and completed as anticipated within allocations of time, personnel, and financial resources? What were the results and the implications for ongoing planning? The financial implications? Is the initiative ongoing or can it be declared complete and removed from the operative implementation program?

As information is gathered, a progress report can be developed; one way to do this is simply to annotate the written plan in a column dedicated to that purpose. The school head will integrate what has or has not been done with ongoing operations at the administrative and faculty levels and report to the board as appropriate at regular intervals. Some items in the implementation program will be the subject of almost constant board discussion and involvement, such as fundraising or capital improvements. Others, for example those that concern the composition, operations, specific responsibilities, and other initiatives unique to the board, will be its responsibility both to implement and to appraise. Still other items will be more remote from board involvement, such as a curriculum study, the development of new course offerings, or revamping cocurricular activities. While the locus of authority will vary for specific items in the implementation program, appraisal of the entire strategic program is the responsibility of the committee so charged and of administrative and board leadership.

At least one caveat here: Many schools I have worked with have achieved remarkable results in implementing plans with little by way of a formal *written* implementation program. Such schools tend to be smaller, have very strong heads, and a high level of trust throughout the school community.

When I first worked with Chesterfield Day School in 1983, it was the St. Louis Montessori Academy, a very special elementary school in a green and rolling suburb of St. Louis. Enrollment was under 200 in grades PK through 6. Children occupied classrooms surrounding a central gym and gathering space in one building; the full-time faculty numbered 11 with an equal number of part-time faculty; the school was run by four administrators; and the annual budget totaled less than $400,000.

The plan the school developed in 1983 targeted the integration of the computer as a tool into the core curriculum (a hot issue in many schools at that time); significant improvement in faculty compensation, benefits, and professional development; more efficient admissions policies that would also increase the student body diversity; a financial aid program; a campus master planning process to address substantial space needs; a development program to include annual giving; creating an endowment fund; and initiating a capital campaign to support many of the elements in the plan.

Progress in every area was noted in a planning session in 1986. At that workshop 22 participants drawn from the school community, many of whom took part in the 1983 meeting, appraised the progress of what by then had become the Chesterfield Day School as a result of examining mission, image, marketing, and public relations issues. After charting what had been accomplished since publishing the '83 plan, which included enrollment growth to 220, adding a wing to the original building, fundraising success, and major evolution in program to anticipate children's needs, the group went to work to reexamine the future and to cast the plan forward another five years.

In the summer of 1992 I was again invited to lead an appraisal and continuous planning workshop for Chesterfield Day School. Exciting changes on the campus were immediately obvious: another handsome building had been built, extensive parking lot and playground space had been added, land had been acquired next door, and renovation of an existing building was underway to house the youngest children. The faculty and staff had grown to 30 FTEs (full time equivalents), enrollment to 255, and the annual budget to $1.5 million. Annual giving and fundraising events average about $120,000 each year and the school has raised $1 million in capital gifts. The head reports that morale within the school has never been higher.

I have highlighted only the most dramatic evidence of CDS's progress in shaping strategy and implementing it. Although trustee and administrative leadership used the evolving strategic plans as a road map and referred often to both the goals and suggestions for implementation contained therein, a formal, written implementation program in addition to the framework of mission, goals, rationales, and suggestions for implementation was not written down in '83, nor in '86. Yet a significant amount of positive action was achieved. During that period the school has had (and still has as of this writing) the same very able and energetic head, there has continued to be a high degree of involvement, ownership, and effective communication regarding expectations throughout the school community, and a sense of a compelling mission in its special approach to educating young children. I think that these factors – the strong continuity, no need to constantly question decisions that had been made as a result of the planning work, and a commitment to the unique nature of the school – maintained the momentum from initial planning through successful execution.

The point is that every school may not need the same degree of formal structure to successfully implement strategic planning; however, larger size and greater complexity tend to increase that need.

Appraisal Intervals

It has proved useful in many schools to hold a full-scale planning workshop every four or five years to augment the work of a committee charged with appraisal and to revitalize the planning process. The focus for this kind of workshop is to build on the planning foundation that has already been laid, emphasizing the continuity of all the planning efforts to date. Agenda items would include:

- an appraisal of what had and had not been achieved since the last plan was originally published
- a list of changes, both internal and external, that must be recognized in the current round of planning
- a participatory process, much like those outlined in the workshop agendas used to create an original plan, to propose updated and new goals, rationales and suggestions for implementation that are responsive to future needs and shared vision as well as to the present climate
- a review of the mission statement with recommendations for any adjustments
- a consensus regarding current strategic priorities
- a plan for designing an updated implementation program, including a method for interaction and communication with the school community in making decisions and taking action based on the strategic plan
- an updated appraisal, feedback and "feed forward" mechanism

Shaping strategy is a continuous course. There is no magic in planning itself. But it is an effective leadership and management tool – especially when it is viewed as a process, not a panacea or an event unrelated to the daily life of a school.

Chapter Seven
Problems and Pitfalls

While many planning principles can be generalized, schools are not identical. Each must analyze and evaluate its own culture and needs in order to design a viable planning process. In this chapter, I will discuss a variety of circumstances that aren't necessarily unique but which represent conditions – I'm tempted to be trendy and use the ever-popular "paradigms" – deserving of recognition and some accommodation.

Developmental Stages in the Life Cycles of Schools

I have found that perhaps the greatest differences among schools, other than the obvious ones of location and type, are to be found in their relative age. Just as schools respond in their educational philosophies and curricula to the developmental ages and needs of children, so schools exhibit different characteristics and needs according to their position in the lifespan of organizations.

There is a considerable body of research and theory about organizational behavior and development. One book that I have found useful is *Corporate Lifecycles: How and Why Corporations Grow and Die and What To Do About It*, by management guru Ichak Adizes, who is described by one of his adherents as "the Darwin of corporate evolution." Adizes echoes others in describing corporate life cycles on the familiar bellshaped curve. On the left are the stages of infancy, childhood growth, and adolescence. On the right are aristocracy, bureaucracy, and eventual death. Just to the left of the top is "prime"– the most desirable stage as a mature but not an aging and stagnating organization. The prime stage is located near but not quite at the zenith to denote that the organization is still growing (not necessarily in size). It is important to note that chronological age alone doesn't characterize an organization. For instance, I have observed that a 30-year-old school can already be exhibiting some of the hallmarks of old age in developmental terms, just as a 100-year-old school can have managed to stay at prime for decades.

Adizes contends that at each stage (each organization will not necessarily go through all) an organizations will have typical problems. Solving them at one level merely prepares an organization for more difficult problems waiting at the next level. For example, organizations in infancy tend to be action oriented. Few policies exist and management is driven by one incredibly dedicated person. The organization is crisis oriented, and financially vulnerable because of inconsistent performance and lack of capitalization. (Think about the rapid rise and demise of many schools related to the fundamentalist religious movement in the 1980s...) The focus is survival; there is simply no time to think and plan. Everyone is involved in an all out, burn-the-candle-at-both-ends effort to keep operations going. While it's probably needed, a full-scale, true long range planning process at this point may just be frustrating. The most efficacious approach is strategic planning that emphasizes the short term so that the organization can test ideas and gain experience.

Along with success, growth and adolescence can bring conflict between the founders and people who joined the organization later, Adizes explains. Also typical are a change in the original vision, new control of management exercised by the board, the development of new rules and policies, and the proliferation of priorities and meetings.

Prime is characterized by Adizes as "... the optimum point on the life cycle curve, where the organization achieves a balance of self control and flexibility." At this point there are working systems and an effective organizational structure, and institutionalized mission and vision. Customer needs are met; plans are made and followed; excellence in performance is predictable. Prime is not without problems, but they tend to be expected and planned for – perhaps there is a cash flow problem, but it isn't a crisis. There are needs for more well-trained people, but professional development programs are planned and funded. A looming problem is avoiding complacency.

The aging side of the cycle signals potential decline, according to Adizes. An organization begins to lose its flexibility, the spirit of creativity and innovation disappears, and an attitude of "if it ain't broke, don't fix it" creeps in. The organization occupies a stable position in the marketplace by now; there is an increasing adherence to precedence and conservative management so that past achievements are not threatened. There are lower expectations for growth, more focus on past achievements than visions of the future, suspicion of change. These attributes can all spiral downward until the organization is moribund.

I think that Adizes' description of the needs and the focus of decision-making in each stage has direct implications for planning in independent schools. The focus for planning in in<u>fan</u>cy, according to Adizes, is on <u>*why*</u> something should be done. What, how, and who are of incidental interest. Following infancy, <u>*what*</u> to do eclipses why. <u>*How* takes over in adolescence.</u> <u>*Who*</u> is the main focus in prime.

I believe that why, what, how, and who must all be elements of a well-crafted plan, even though tendencies may exist to emphasize one over another in a specific life cycle stage. There are usually no clear-cut rites of passage from stage to stage, and organizations can experience the problems of more than one growth stage at any given time.

The organizational developmental approach is interesting to me as applied to independent schools, and it is easy to adapt Adizes' corporate models. When considering the growth stage of a given school according to Adizes' theories, appropriate planning methodology will differ. Chesterfield Day School's planning experience, highlighted in Chapter Six, exemplifies in many ways that of a school in early planned growth stages moving into prime. Older, larger, longer-established schools such as Germantown Academy will take a somewhat different, usually more formal and institutionalized tack to respond to the challenges particular to them. Neither one method nor the other is "right" *per se*; they differ as needs differ. I believe that the very process of shaping future strategy and programming action accordingly helps a school reach and remain at prime.

Planning and the Accreditation Process

There is rarely a perfect time to plan. The school calendar is always full; everyone is already at capacity doing daily tasks. But the school is due to enter into the reaccreditation process. Many schools have asked me how that process and planning might conflict or converge. The reaccreditation self-study inevitably directs schools to collect a great variety of data, much of which is directly useful in strategic planning. But the process does not substitute for planning, as some have suggested, since its appropriate and stated focus is largely internal, concentrates on past performance, assesses a school according to its existing mission statement, and centers around a visit (or reality check) by a group of peers. These visitors are, in a sense, performing an audit: Is the school performing according to the findings in the self-study? They are charged with making very specific recommendations in light of their experience. Planning, on the other hand, is concerned with issues of future strategic intent, external as well as internal – with judging the relevance of the stated mission to tomorrow, and, in the broadest sense, with the vision for the next century.

The question to consider in deciding whether to engage both processes in proximity is not so much their respective focuses – which I see as complementary, "where we've been," as opposed to "where we choose to go" – but a question of institutional energy. Many people who must be involved in one process may also bear responsibilities in the other. Can that be managed to avoid burnout?

Planning and Crisis

Neil Cullen's narrative of Andover's approach to threatening financial realities is a superb example of how to use the tenets of effective planning (education, participation, gathering data, developing ownership in a plan of action) to resolve difficult immediate issues.

Another useful example is that of the Southfield School in Shreveport, Louisiana. Beginning its existence as an elementary school in the 1930s, Southfield added upper grades in the early '70s to meet a perceived community demand. Faced in subsequent years with a deteriorating local economy, repeated changes in leadership, and reduced expectations, Southfield was forced to examine the increasingly negative financial impact of upper school operations on the relatively healthy elementary division. Under the leadership of a new school head, Southfield used the basic planning process I have described to examine future options and to make a recommendation to the board about the viability of continuing to operate the upper division. That recommendation was only one of a set of integrated goals relating to the whole school. In an honest, searching, sometimes painful weekend workshop in which board members, administration, faculty, and other parents participated (all of whom would be directly affected), consensus was reached to recommend discontinuing the upper school. The decision was not an easy one as considerable resources of money, time, energy, and commitment had been devoted to trying to make it a success. The recognition that forces outside Southfield's control made success for such a venture virtually impossible at the time was cold comfort, I am sure. The planning process served as a vehicle to place the problem in a broader context, thereby assisting to revamp the vision of the school within its stated mission.

Restructuring and "Downsizing"

Schools in the "oil patch" are not alone in scrutinizing the financial realities of a declining enrollment pool and a decrease in earned income and philanthropic support. Southfield is just one of many schools that has been forced to examine how to continue to fulfill the mandates of their missions. Several years ago I worked with a New England boarding school facing the pressures caused by a shrinking enrollment. In several preceding years the school had made all the "easy" cuts – in other words, those that did not reduce faculty and staff. Recognizing that trends looked as if they would continue downward for a few years to come, school leadership asked me to help navigate through a "downsizing" procedure. What we discovered was that everything could not be subject to decreased support. Marketing and fundraising programs had to be increased if the school's lifeblood was to continue to flow. Instead of any across-the-board reductions, the analysis centered on areas to be added or enhanced, those to be maintained, and those to be reduced or eliminated.

There is a marked tendency in independent schools to add to program, but rarely to take anything away. I think every school would be well advised to examine its curriculum from time to time with an eye to adding *only* if something commensurate can be deleted. Faculty often state quite truthfully that there is too much to accomplish in too little time. In program as in all else, difficult decisions must be faced about program proliferation in light of centrality to mission.

Having worked with quite a number of businesses and large institutions outside the independent school world, I have found it germane to talk not of "downsizing" but of "restructuring" or "rightsizing." This is not merely a case of semantics nor of trying to make difficult decisions more palatable. Rather it speaks to the issue of flexibility, considered in many industries to be a crucial competitive advantage. Developing alternate scenarios as part of financial planning and forecasting is a good way to anticipate "rightsizing" long before it is thrust upon you.

When Capital Projects Take Over
Plant and facilities needs have a way of firing the imagination and becoming the focal point of many a planning initiative. Planning doesn't always lead to new buildings and capital campaigns to finance them, but neither is that phenomenon uncommon. As a strategic planning issue, physical facilities ideally would be seen as a function of program priorities, not the reverse. A campus master plan that is driven by a carefully developed strategic plan can be a tremendous impetus to developing a case statement for a capital campaign. Such a plan is also extremely useful in negotiating with a donor who would like to give a school a named, single-function building that it doesn't want.

If a school spends all its energy for a period of time in constructing buildings, once those are celebrated and dedicated attention should be redirected through an appraisal and a continuous planning agenda to other important items that may have been in abeyance.

Strategic Planning and a Change in School Heads

Changes in leadership, either planned or unplanned, dictate some prescriptive measures in a planning cycle. Changes in board leadership are routine every several years; continuity at the board level and a dynamic planning process ensure that a school takes changes in board leadership in stride. A change in the headship may be a different matter. Schools often decide to enter a new round of planning as part of a managed succession; the retirement of the head or the decision of the sitting head to seek another position provides an opportunity for a school to take stock collectively. A planning process can be used very advantageously to assess the strengths of the institution, and determine general directions and goals that will help identify the experience level, skills, and personal characteristics of potential candidates. A participatory planning process can also lessen the anxieties felt throughout a school during a time of uncertainty.

One caution: Schools should remember that there must to be ways for the incoming leader to have a role in shaping strategy – particularly in the implementation programming. However, if the strategic framework has been outlined, it will be much easier for schools and head candidates to clarify and match expectations.

Planning and Religious Schools

Governance in schools connected to religious organizations such as churches and synagogues can range from merely complex to absolutely Byzantine. Relevant components include the ownership of assets, nominal and actual school administrative leadership by church personnel, institutional politics, turf, space allocation, and what entity has final authority over school operations (The board? The vestry? The diocese?). A planning effort must recognize these interconnected factors in every aspect of a planning process, including the leadership of the process, the workshop participants, the drafting team members, internal and external communications, and the locus of authority to approve recommendations and decisions.

Planning in Schools with a Pattern of Dysfunctional Behavior

Although I have repeatedly underscored the essential nature of planning as a *process,* it has been used in some instances as a kind of intervention. What comes to mind is the type of school that has earned the reputation, deservedly or not, for being a revolving door for heads, or one in which the parents, the board, or the faculty are perceived as inappropriately "running the school." Because people representing the whole school community are brought together in a process that examines how participants want a school to function in the future and that does not dwell on fault-finding and the past, there is a reasonable chance that destructive institutional behavior can be identified and incremental steps for constructive change explored.

In many instances, I think the choice to use outside consulting and facilitation for planning is optional. In the kinds of dysfunctional situations in this category, the assistance of an experienced, impartial outside professional is a must.

Resistance to Change or The "If It Ain't Broke..." Syndrome

Listening to consultant Joel A. Barker, author of *Future Edge: Discovering the New Paradigms of Success,* address a conference of health care providers helped crystallize for me many observations I've made about how people consider change.

Organizations generally exist and operate in a state of equilibrium. The culture, predictable patterns, and daily habits within a school allow it to function. In independent schools, as in organizations where Barker has done research, innovation is often resisted – think about trying to revamp the curriculum. A crisis, on the other hand, encourages innovation – think about Southfield, or a forced downsizing or mobilizing after a natural disaster.

Barker's point is that the amount of disequilibrium produced by innovation is disproportionate to the perceived change an innovation will create, not necessarily to the real change it creates. Therefore, in attempting to foster a positive climate for change, one must always look at innovation and its potential impact from the point of view and sense of security of those who will be affected. The innovator's point of view, Barker states flatly, is irrelevant.

Independent schools by their very nature are well suited to innovate once the will to do so has been forged. Taking advantage of the national mood to improve education, new research about learning, and lessons about educational effectiveness in other cultures and countries are just a few motivators for potential change. Yet there is a lingering "if it ain't broke…" mentality in many places. How can you deal with changing even the daily schedule, let alone grapple with some of the larger educational issues of the day?

Based on research by Dr. Everett Rogers and James R. Bright, Barker has developed a list of practical tactics to help minimize resistance to innovation. Because I think the ideas are essential in implementing a strategic plan, I have paraphrased those I consider most relevant to independent schools in this final checklist:

- A person whom change will affect should easily be able to see the advantages of that change over current methods and practices.
- If an idea is perceived as fitting in with what's already being done and it can be described in familiar vocabulary, the chances of its acceptance improve (evolutionary change).
- Supporting activities for the innovation should be kept simple, although the innovation itself may be complex ("user-friendliness").
- If an innovation can be tried one step at a time, the chances for acceptance of the overall change are higher (incremental change).
- The credibility and trustworthiness of the innovator are critical to acceptance of change.
- Consider the consequences of failure and whether or not there is a safety net; the less potential *personal* jeopardy there is, the higher the degree of acceptance for innovation.

Finally, I would add to Barker's list:

- The higher the degree of participation throughout an organization in creating innovation, the greater the degree not only of acceptance, but also of success.

These tactics to minimize resistance lead me back to where I began, just as a planning process recycles, to reinforce the power of shared vision in shaping a successful strategic plan.

Afterword

While I was struggling to pull together a final draft of this book, wondering already (in the best spirit of what I have described in these pages) how I might wish to revise it in a year or two, I attended a workshop given by my friend and colleague Dick Ireland (See Chapter Two.)

As far as I know, Dick was unaware of my writing project. But as if he sensed my need for a summation, he described strategic planning as a unified approach to the future. Further, he said that a successful plan must be sustainable, and that building consensus around vision and mission is the critical element in both that unity and its sustainability.

One of the most significant movements in business and industrial circles today is based on the core values of what is called "total quality management," evolving into "continuous quality improvement," which is in turn metamorphosing into whatever the next generation of theory and practice will be called.

Those core values are timeless: participation, teamwork, ownership, empowerment, and drawing out individual hidden knowledge, as well as measurement, gathering data to support or counter opinion, an incremental approach to improvement and change, and taking action at appropriate levels. I am struck by the similarity of such motivating ideas to those I have discussed in relationship to planning.

Shaping strategy that will be effective for an independent school must be driven by both the head and the heart. Crafting a successful plan will not separate the analytical and the creative. The planning process – the journey itself – will reinforce the unity and sense of shared purpose so often found in independent schools.

Bibliography

Adizes, Ichak. *Corporate Lifecycles: How and Why Corporations Grow and Die and What To Do About It.* Englewood Cliffs, New Jersey: Prentice Hall, 1988.

Barker, Joel A. *Future Edge: Discovering the New Paradigms of Success.* New York: William Morrow and Company, Inc., 1992.

Benveniste, Gary. *Mastering the Politics of Planning.* San Francisco: Jossey-Bass, 1989.

Chait, Richard P., Thomas P. Holland and Barbara E. Taylor. *The Effective Board of Trustees.* New York: Macmillan Publishing Company, 1991.

Frances, Carol, George Huxel, Joel W. Meyerson and Dabney G. Park, Jr. *Strategic Decision Making: Key Questions and Indicators for Trustees.* Washington, D.C.: Association of Governing Boards of Universities and Colleges, 1987.

Mintzberg, Henry. *Mintzberg on Management: Inside Our Strange World of Organizations.* New York: The Free Press, 1989.

Schwartz, Peter. *The Art of the Long View: Planning for the Future in an Uncertain World*. New York: Doubleday, 1991.

Senge, Peter M. *The Fifth Discipline: The Art & Practice of the Learning Organization*. New York: Doubleday, 1990.

Stanton, Barbara Hadley. *Trustee Handbook, 6th ed.* Boston: National Association of Independent Schools, 1989.

Taylor, Barbara E., Joel W. Meyerson, Louis R. Morrell and Dabney G. Park, Jr. *Strategic Analysis: Using Comparative Data to Understand Your Institution*. Washington, D.C.: Association of Governing Boards of Universities and Colleges, 1991.

Appendices

Appendix A: *Outline of the Strategic Planning Process*
Strategic Planning Chart

Appendix B: *Sample Set of Planning Documents*
Germantown Academy
Fort Washington, Pennsylvania

Appendix C: *Sample Implementation Program*
St. Martin's Episcopal School
Metairie, Louisiana

Appendix D: *Sample Computerized Implementation Program*
Mary Institute, St. Louis, Missouri

Appendix A

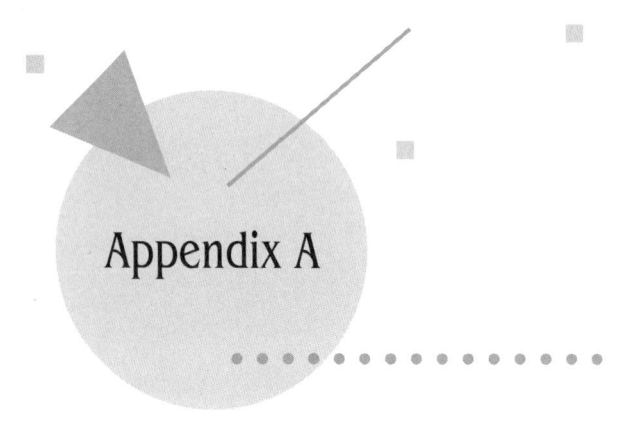

Outline of the Strategic Planning Process

I. **Preparing for a cycle of planning**
   A. *Designing the process and calendar*
   B. *Designating leadership and participants*
   C. *Developing background data*
   D. *Determining research needs*
   E. *Making logistical arrangements*
   F. *Communicating with the school community*
   G. *Implementing the decisions made in this phase*

II. **Shaping a strategic plan**
   A. *Analyzing background data*
   B. *Brainstorming external factors that may impact the school in the future*
   C. *Brainstorming school topics to be considered*
   D. *Envisioning the school in the future*

E. *Building consensus*
   F. *Defining policy goals and supporting information*
   G. *Appraising the mission statement*
   H. *Identifying strategic priorities*
   I. *Preparing and presenting a draft report*
   J. *Communicating with the school community*

III. Implementing the strategic plan
   A. *Designing the implementation program*
   B. *Integrating with budgeting and long-range financial planning*
   C. *Making strategic decisions and setting priorities*
   D. *Communicating with the school community*
   E. *Appraising and updating the implementation program*

IV. Renewing the strategic plan
   A. *Reassessing the existing strategic plan*
   B. *Revitalizing the planning process and entering a new cycle of planning*
   C. *Shaping new strategy*

Shaping Strategy

The Strategic Planning Process

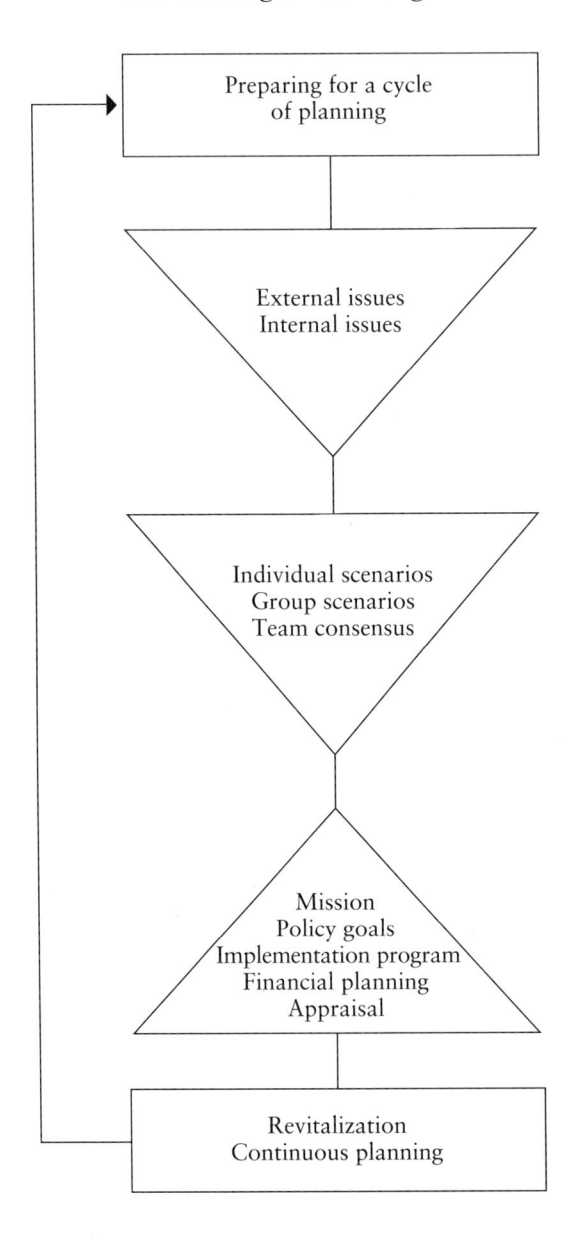

```
Preparing for a cycle
of planning

External issues
Internal issues

Individual scenarios
Group scenarios
Team consensus

Mission
Policy goals
Implementation program
Financial planning
Appraisal

Revitalization
Continuous planning
```

Appendix B

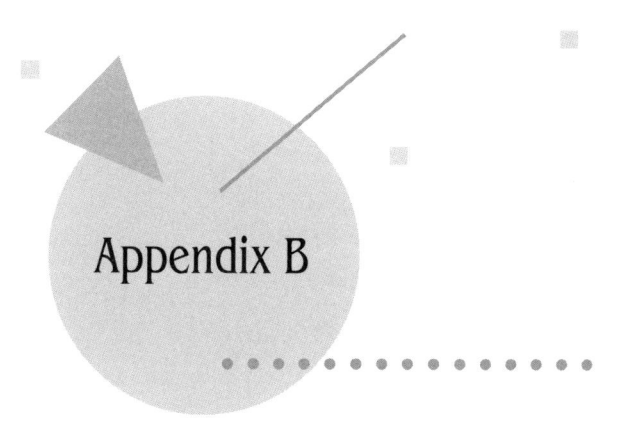

Sample Set of Planning Documents
Germantown Academy
Fort Washington, Pennsylvania

GERMANTOWN ACADEMY

Fort Washington, Pennsylvania
Founded 1759

May 15, 1992

Dear Parents:

In lieu of the Headmaster's usual spring letter informing you of recent events at school, we are delighted to present Germantown Academy's Strategic Plan, the result of an intense and inclusive planning process begun last August. Our expectation is that the Strategic Plan will serve as the guide to the Academy's future. With this document comes an invitation to attend an open meeting on Tuesday, June 2, 1992, at 7:00 p.m., when we will gather in the Arts Center to discuss, as a community, this multifaceted vision of the Academy's future.

Many individuals spent countless hours creating this Strategic Plan. Our meetings were inspiring as we examined all areas of school life, developed comprehensive goals pertaining to each, and established strategies for accomplishing those goals. We discovered that we shared a remarkable consensus regarding the Academy's educational mission. In this draft of the Plan, we have also included the major recommendations of two other projects completed this year, the Multicultural Assessment Plan and the Sixth Grade Study.

Hand-in-hand with the development of the Strategic Plan comes a review of the Academy's Mission Statement. That document is reflective of the goals listed in the Strategic Plan. The revised Mission Statement is still very much "in process," and is currently being refined in discussions with faculty and trustees. By early fall we expect to have it completed and approved by the Board. Once that is done, we will publish and send to everyone in the G.A. community a formal version of the updated Strategic Plan, incorporating the newly revised Mission Statement.

As you will see from reading all of the enclosed information, it has been a very productive year for Germantown Academy. We are appreciative of the work of so many people; without their efforts, the creation of the Strategic Plan would not have been possible. Special thanks go to Jane Deming, Trustee and Chair of the Strategic Planning Steering Committee, and Suzie Perot, Director of Studies, whose guidance and leadership helped us to put into words the vision we shared for the Strategic Plan.

We are an excellent school right now working to be an exceptional school in the near future. We hope that you will share our enthusiasm for the Academy's future and will join us on June 2. Your thoughts and perspective on the Strategic Plan are very important to us; please take a moment to respond to the Plan by using the enclosed comment sheet. If you are able to attend the June 2 meeting, please call Peggy Jones by May 29.

We look forward to your response.

Best wishes,

James W. Connor   *Christopher J. Davis*
Headmaster   President, Board of Trustees

P.S. If you cannot be with us at the June 2 meeting but would like a time to discuss your thoughts regarding the Strategic Plan, don't hesitate to call. A mutually convenient time to talk with us or one of the members of the Steering Committee can be arranged.

Comment Sheet

For parents to respond in writing to the Strategic Plan
We are sincerely interested in learning of your reactions to the Strategic Plan. Please take a moment to share with us your thoughts about the Plan. Your responses will be used to help us formulate the agenda for the June 2 meeting. Please return this sheet to Jim Connor, Headmaster, c/o Germantown Academy.

Signature (optional)

Strategic Planning
An Overview of a Dynamic and Inclusive Process

Germantown Academy is a school that, for many years, has embraced continuing self-evaluation as a vital ingredient in creating a first class educational experience for students. In keeping with that philosophy, the school directed a tremendous amount of energy toward the creation of a Strategic Plan to guide the work of the Academy over the next several years.

We began the Strategic Plan process with four parameters in mind. First, we did not see the Strategic Plan as a vehicle for drastic changes in direction, but rather an opportunity to achieve a more focused approach to developing plans for various areas of school life. Second, we wanted to include the perspectives of trustees, faculty, parents, students, and alumni at all stages of the development of the Strategic Plan. Third, we wanted to fold into the Strategic Plan the work of two other projects, the Multicultural Assessment Plan and the Sixth Grade Study. Fourth, we desired a plan that would be a dynamic blueprint for the Academy's future, yet that would be flexible enough to allow for alterations as the school progressed towards achieving the initial goals.

To assist our efforts, we engaged the help of Susan C. Stone, a highly respected consultant in the field of long range and strategic planning. Jane Deming, Trustee, and Suzie Perot, the Academy's Director of Studies, orchestrated the planning process, and established a Planning Committee of 42 dedicated individuals (consisting of parents, alumni, trustees, and faculty members) who assembled for an intense three day workshop prior to the beginning of the '91-'92 academic year. At the workshop, we shared our perceptions of the impact of a host of internal, external, social, economic, and educational forces on the Academy's future.

We honed our dreams into viable goals and discussed a wealth of strategies for achieving those goals.

Then, during the fall, a Steering Committee of 12 people sifted through the mountains of data and presented the resulting compilation of proposed goals and strategies for approval at the trustees' November meeting. In December, the trustees, faculty, Parents' Executive Committee, Alumni Executive Committee, and students (over 100 individuals strong) met to prioritize the strategies for meeting the approved goals. Using this information, the Steering Committee then spent the winter refining and finalizing the Strategic Plan.

As noted previously, both the Multicultural Assessment Plan (MAP) study and the Sixth Grade Study were conducted concurrently with the strategic planning process. The MAP study, based on the NAIS. (National Association of Independent Schools) endorsed self-assessment document, offered G.A. an indepth opportunity to assess how the school has addressed and will address the issue of education in a multicultural society. Co-chairing the MAP study were faculty members Ellen Harris, Director of Lower School Admission, Kendall Mattern, Upper School History teacher, and Joe Rozak, Upper School Science teacher. Preparations for MAP began nearly two years ago; the study itself took place from September through November. In January, a visiting committee, consisting of experienced independent school educators, under the auspices of NAIS, spent three days at G.A. to assess for themselves the findings gleaned from our selfstudy. Their report was received in late March and discussed at length by the trustees, faculty, Parents' Committee, Alumni Board, and student representatives at the April Joint Trustee Faculty meeting. The input generated from that gathering helped us reach an understanding on which recommendations should become part of the Strategic Plan. It is our expectation that the implementation of the recommendations will further enhance the high academic standards developed by the Academy through the years.

The Sixth Grade Study was of similar scope, involving countless hours of deliberate, thoughtful research and discussion. A Steering Committee of faculty, parents, and trustees set out to study the desirability of moving the sixth grade to Middle School. After thorough review of the available research and discussions with students and parents, the resulting report to the trustees in February recommended that the educational and social needs of adolescents aged 11-14 would be better served in a similar setting, provided that the setting itself was appropriate. The trustees accepted this recommendation and charged the Sixth Grade Committee, chaired by Assistant Middle School Head Emily Wagner, with developing a proposal to address the physical space and curricular needs involved in making the Middle School setting appropriate for the inclusion of sixth graders. The committee expects to report its findings to the Board by next December.

Because of the work of so many people during this past year, Germantown Academy has charted its directions for the foreseeable future. The process of engaging in strategic planning has already produced recognizable results; many of the strategies highlighted are being implemented. All of us at G.A.– trustees, administration, faculty, and parents – are fully committed to implementing the Strategic Plan in a timely fashion. Of equal importance is our collective commitment to making this Strategic Plan a living, breathing plan – subject to renewal and revision each year.

The Strategic Plan of Germantown Academy

The Academic Program

Germantown Academy will offer pre-kindergarten through 12th grade students a college preparatory program rooted in the tradition of the liberal arts and the development needs of the whole child. Our purposes will be to engage students in the exploration and connection of information and ideas that matter; to ensure that they practice and master, with guidance, those processes of learning and habits of mind necessary to a thoughtful life; and to develop in them a strong sense of competence and a capacity to live and work well with others. We will be dedicated to excellence in all that we do and strive to be the school of choice within our community.

Strategies

- Improve the integration of the curriculum by content and by skill:

    Teach reading and writing across all grade levels and in all fields of study

    Increase interdisciplinary work at all levels of the school

    Define the habits of mind most crucial to students' learning at all levels of the school

- Implement the findings from recent research and pedagogy:

    Increase the use of the model of student as worker, teacher as coach

    Develop a repertoire of cooperative learning strategies to use with students at all grade levels across all disciplines

    Develop, within all courses, methods for teaching to students' various learning styles

- Research and implement the best use of technology in the curriculum, pre-kindergarten through grade twelve
- Incorporate a multicultural perspective in all fields of study across all grade levels
- Integrate the sixth grade and the current Middle School curricula in preparation for the move of the sixth grade to Middle School
- Study the development of a Lower School foreign language program

The Administration

Germantown Academy will attract and retain an outstanding and dedicated group of capable, creative, and sensitive administrative leaders and the appropriate staff support. Regular assessments of the school's performance and continuing efforts to improve the quality of its programs will be one of the administration's highest priorities.

Strategies
- Identify the best administrative and staff support system for each division
- Attract administrators from diverse ethnic backgrounds, as openings occur
- Raise the administrative salaries to be among the highest of independent schools in the area and to the 90th percentile of NAIS schools
- Implement an evaluation system for administrators
- Increase the use of technology for administrative use

Admissions

Germantown Academy will enroll and retain a student body of approximately 1000 students of average to superior intellectual abilities. The school will seek students with a broad range of cultural backgrounds, talents, and interests who are committed to learning and who will be good citizens in and out of school.

Strategies

- Increase outreach to students from diverse ethnic, religious, and socio-economic backgrounds
- Identify specific groups and geographic areas for recruiting
- Protect and increase, as possible, the financial aid budget
- Evaluate competitive academic scholarships as an effective recruiting tool for admission
- Promote the G.A. Ambassadors program
- Increase awareness of G.A. in the international community

The Alumni

Germantown Academy will appreciate its alumni as a critical constituency of the school and more aggressively cultivate a mutually beneficial relationship with them.

Strategies

- Increase involvement of alumni in friend-raising and fundraising
- Develop programs to bring alumni back to campus

- Increase outreach to alumni of diverse racial and ethnic backgrounds; invite them to be resources in admission efforts, role models for students, and guest speakers
- Develop in Upper School students a deeper understanding of their future responsibilities as alumni
- Increase alumni participation in Annual Giving to 40 percent
- Increase alumni giving to make-up one quarter of total Annual Giving
- Increase involvement of faculty in alumni activities
- Publish an updated Alumni Directory every five years

Development

Germantown Academy will be committed to the development of financial resources, other than tuition, to fulfill the mission of the school and to fund the goals of the Strategic Plan. The school will seek funds through annual and capital giving to meet the needs for financial aid, merit scholarships, higher salaries and benefits, rising operating costs, specific program expenses, plant maintenance, and debt arising from past capital expenditures.

Strategies
- Increase total annual giving from all sources to 6 percent of the operating budget
- Initiate a feasibility study for a possible Capital Campaign
- Develop relationships with foundations and corporations
- Develop a planned giving program
- Engage a significantly larger percentage of all constituencies in fundraising for the school

The Faculty

Germantown Academy will attract and retain an outstanding and dedicated faculty of diverse backgrounds and complementary talents who will be excellent teachers and role models for students, who will grow personally and professionally, and who will contribute to the overall life of the school.

Strategies

- Raise salaries and benefits to be among the highest of independent schools in the area and at the 90th percentile of NAIS schools
- Expand the pool of applicants from diverse racial and ethnic backgrounds
- Increase faculty in-service at all levels of the school with regard to learning styles and learning differences, cooperative learning, interdisciplinary study, and technology
- Develop educational programs to assist faculty/administrators in dealing with issues of diversity
- Set standards for and expand faculty professional growth (workshops, graduate study, etc.)
- Revise the faculty evaluation system to make it appropriate to the needs of each school division
- Complete the feasibility study for developing a financially self-sustaining on-site day care facility

Finances

Germantown Academy will be committed to sound financial planning. In its financial planning, the school will balance the competing needs for increased compensation, need-based financial aid, general operating costs, specific program expenses, plant maintenance, and affordable tuitions. It will exercise fiscal discipline in all areas.

Strategies
- Do a three-to-five year financial plan
- Investigate ways to make G.A. more affordable to the middle class
- Study the long term impact of faculty/staff full tuition remission for faculty/staff hired in the future
- Strengthen the summer programs and the auxiliary enterprises of school
- Develop and enforce the policies regarding scheduled tuition payment
- Explore alternative tuition models as part of the three-to-five year financial plan

Governance

The Board of Trustees will be composed of a broad range of diverse and talented individuals who represent a balance of expertise, experience, and constituencies. Election to and membership on the Board shall require visible dedication to the school and a commitment to share wisdom, work, and/or wealth in pursuit of the mission and goals of the school.

Strategies
- Educate trustees more fully about the nature of independent education and operations of the school
- Continue joint faculty/trustee meetings and trustee/faculty committee work
- Recruit trustees from outside the G.A. community
- Resolve the issue of full faculty membership on the Board
- Actively involve every trustee in raising money for the school
- Lengthen terms for parent representatives from one year to two years
- Develop candidates for the Board by assessing their performance on Board Committees
- Establish an Advisory Board that meets bi-annually to offer advice and assistance

The Parents

Germantown Academy will forge strong partnerships with parents that will be enhanced by mutual trust and direct communication. The school and parents will cooperate in the ethical, academic, artistic, athletic, and civil development of students, and for the overall benefit of the school.

Strategies
- Recognize parental support in publications and school gatherings
- Educate parents regarding multicultural issues and changing family structures
- Invite parents of different cultural backgrounds to share their areas of expertise with students and faculty

- Develop a network to communicate clearly the school's expectations for tone of behavior and citizenship of students
- Clarify avenues for expressions of parental concerns and the school's response
- Make parents more aware of the financial needs of the school and, conversely, make the school more aware of the financial needs of parents
- Define and develop a group of parent volunteers to help with administrative needs of the school
- Involve parents in career days

The Physical Plant

Germantown Academy enjoys the benefit of an excellent physical plant and will strive to maintain its facilities in a manner that contributes to the success of our overall goals.

Strategies

- Fund the Academy's long-term maintenance requirements on an annual basis
- Evaluate the benefits of an increased use of the school's facilities by outside groups
- Review policies regarding the rental use of facilities
- Study the feasibility of external access for the physically challenged
- Study the school's maintenance and clean-up requirements and hire sufficient staff to meet them
- Heighten the awareness of environmental concerns
- Ensure that all federal, state, and local guidelines are met with reference to the campus

- Consider retaining an architect to develop a Campus Plan that ensures the logical use of our present facilities to meet better the program and administrative needs of the school

The Student Body

Germantown Academy will promote children's ethical, intellectual, and physical growth. Through its programs, the school will encourage students to develop their talents, to address their shortcomings, and to be responsible for their education. It will offer to students diverse opportunities for leadership and for working individually and cooperatively to shape positive changes in the school and in their own lives. The school will expect that students be good citizens in and out of school.

Strategies
- Continue to expand opportunities for student leadership
- Communicate on a regular basis the expectations for tone of behavior and for citizenship
- Pursue an Honor Code for Upper School students
- Include students on relevant standing committees
- Make all students more aware of the environmental needs on campus
- Create a discretionary fund so that all students will have financial access to special programs beyond the normal scope of the school's daily program
- Improve the counseling/guidance services for students from diverse racial and ethnic backgrounds
- Provide students with increased opportunities for discussing multicultural attitudes

Appendix B

Germantown Academy
Implementation Grid

1. *Program Goal:*

Germantown Academy will offer Pre-Kindergarten through Twelfth Grade students a college preparatory program rooted in the tradition of the liberal arts and the developmental needs of the whole child. Our purposes will be to engage students in the exploration and connection of information and ideas that matter, to ensure that they practice and master, with guidance, those processes of learning and habits of mind necessary to a thoughtful life, and to develop in them a strong sense of competence and a capacity to live and work well with others. We will be dedicated to excellence in all that we do and strive to be the school of choice within our community.

Implementation:

Action	Responsibility	Initiation Date	Report Date	Completion Date	Resources Needed	Progress
Ia. Improve the integration of curriculum in Pre K-12, by content and by skill.	Curriculum Committee, Director of Studies, Dept. Heads, Coordinators	Underway	Annual	On-going	Inservice/ workshop $	
Ib. Pay close attention to reading/writing across the curriculum	Reading Steering Committee		Annual	On-going	Inservice $	
II. Keep up-to-date with and implement the best pedagogy with regard to content and students' needs.	Curriculum Committee, Dept. Heads and Coordinators	Underway	Annual	On-going	Inservice/ Workshop $ Travel $	
IIIa. Ensure curriculum is kept current with advances in technology.	Dept. Heads/ Coordinators	Fall '92	Annual	On-going	Inservice Workshop/ Travel $	
IIIb. Develop and implement a school-wide program which integrates technology, pedagogy, and curriculum.	Curriculum Committee, Technology Committee, Dept. Head Coordinators	Spring '92	Spring '93, Fall '93, Spring '94	'94-'95	Inservice/ Workshop $ Travel $ Major Capital and program $	

139

Shaping Strategy

2. *Program Goal:*

Germantown Academy will offer Pre-Kindergarten through Twelfth Grade students a college preparatory program rooted in the tradition of the liberal arts and the developmental needs of the whole child. Our purposes will be to engage students in the exploration and connection of information and ideas that matter, to ensure that they practice and master, with guidance, those processes of learning and habits of mind necessary to a thoughtful life, and to develop in them a strong sense of competence and a capacity to live and work well with others. We will be dedicated to excellence in all that we do and strive to be the school of choice within our community.

Implementation:

Action	Responsibility	Initiation Date	Report Date	Completion Date	Resources Needed	Progress
IV. Investigate financial and logistical implications of approved recommendation to move 6th grade to H.S.	Middle School Study Committee	Spring '92	Fall '92		$ Capital Investment	
V. Investigate and respond to recommendations from MAP selfstudy and report of MAP visiting teams.	Curriculum Committee Dept. Heads, Coordinators	Fall '92	Annual	On-going	Inservice $	
VI. Study the development of Lower School foreign language program	Curriculum Committee, Foreign Language Department, Heads of School	Spring '93	Winter '94			

Appendix B

3. *Admissions Goal:*

Germantown Academy will enroll and retain a student body of approximately 1000 students of average to superior intellectual abilities. The school will seek students with a broad range of backgrounds, talents, and interests who are committed to learning and who will be good citizens in and out of school.

Implementation:

Action	Responsibility	Initiation Date	Report Date	Completion Date	Resources Needed	Progress
I. Implement appropriate recommendations from MAP	Directors of Admissions	Fall '92	Spring '93	On-going	Financial Aid Endowed Financial Aid	
II. Identify and target specific groups and geographic areas	Directors of Admissions	Underway	Annual	On-going		
III. Publish a brochure on affordability	Director of Finance	Fall '92		Spring '93	$1-3,000	
IV. Evaluate competitive academic scholarships as an effective recruiting tool for admissions	Admissions Committee, Marketing Committee	Fall '92	Spring '93		Endowed Fund of $745,000 for 4 scholarships (if deemed an important tool.)	
V. Promote GA Ambassadors program	Directors of Admissions and Parents' Committee	Underway	Annual	On-going		
VI. Increase awareness of GA in international community	Directors of Admissions	Underway	Annual	On-going		
VII. Update Viewbook	Development, Admissions, and Marketing Committees	Spring '92 (Interim)		Every 3-5 yrs.	$40,000 for full version $9,000 for interim	

Shaping Strategy

4. Students Goal:

Germantown Academy will promote children's ethical, intellectual, and physical growth. Through its programs, the school will encourage students to develop their talents, to address their shortcomings, and to be responsible for their education. It will offer students diverse opportunities for leadership and for working individually and cooperatively to shape positive change in the school and their own lives. The school will expect that students be good citizens in and out of school.

Implementation:

Action	Responsibility	Initiation Date	Report Date	Completion Date	Resources Needed	Progress
I. Develop a network to communicate expectations for tone of behavior and for citizenship expected of students.	School Heads, Deans and Heads of Forms, Parents' Committee	Winter '92	Annual	On-going		
II. Continue to expand opportunities for student leadership	Division Heads, Deans, Head of Form	Underway	Annual	On-going		
III. Pursue Honor Code for Upper School students	SFAC/Head of Upper School	Underway	Spring '92	Spring '93		
IV. Include students on relevant standing committees	School Heads	Underway	Annual	On-going		
V. Make all students more aware of environmental needs on campus	Head of Upper School, SFAC, Lower and Middle School Student Councils	Fall '92	Spring '93	On-going		
VI. Evaluate and implement recommendations from MAP	School Heads SFAC, Middle School Student Council	Fall '92	Spring '93	On-going		

Appendix B

5. *Faculty Goal:*

Germantown Academy will attract and retain an outstanding and dedicated faculty of diverse backgrounds and complementary talents who will be excellent teachers and role models for students, who will grow personally and professionally, and who will contribute to the overall life of the school.

Implementation:

Action	Responsibility	Initiation Date	Report Date	Completion Date	Resources Needed	Progress
I. Raise salaries and benefits to be among highest of I.S.' in the area and at the 90th percentile of NAIS schools	Trustees	Underway	Annual	1996	$ from operating budget	
II. Expand pool of minority applicants	Dean of Faculty, Headmaster, School Heads, Dept. Heads	Underway	Annual	On-going		
III. Increase faculty inservice (school-based)	Director of Studies, Dean Faculty, School Heads	Fall '92	Annual	On-going	$	
IV. Set standards for and expand faculty professional growth (workshops, graduate study)	Headmaster and School Heads	Spring '93	Annual	On-going	$	
V. Revise faculty evaluation to make appropriate to each division of the school	School Heads and Faculty Concerns Committee	Underway	Spring '93	Spring '93		
VI. Complete study on feasibility of developing a financially self-sustaining onsite day care facility	Faculty Concerns Committee, Personnel Committee	Underway	Spring '92	As soon as feasible	$100,000-$150,000	

Shaping Strategy

6. *Parents Goal:*

Germantown Academy will forge strong partnerships which will be informed by mutual trust and direct communication. The school and parents will cooperate in the ethical, academic, artistic, athletic, and civil development of students, and for the overall benefit of the school.

Implementation: Action	Responsibility	Initiation Date	Report Date	Completion Date	Resources Needed	Progress
I. Recognition in publications and school gatherings of parental support	Parents' Committee, Development Office	Underway	Annual	On-going		
II. Education for parents RE diversity and changing family structures	Parents' Committee and Counselor, Deans, Division Heads	'92-'93	Annual	On-going		
III. Develop a network to communicate clearly the school's expectations for tone of behavior and citizenship of students	Parents' Committee, Heads of School, Deans, Heads of Form	Fall '92	Winter '93	On-going		
IV. Clarify avenues for expressions of parental concerns and school's concerns	Parents' Committee, Deans, Heads of School, Heads of Form, Headmaster	'92-'93	Spring '93	On-going		
V. Make parents more aware of the financial needs of the school and school more aware of financial needs of parents	Parents' Committee Development Office	Fall '92	Annual	On-going		
VI. Define and develop a group of parents to volunteer to help with administrative needs of school	Parents' Committee and Administrative Team	Fall '92	Annual	On-going		
VII. Involve parents in career days	Parents' Committee, Development Office	Next career day				

Appendix B

7. Administration Goal:

Germantown Academy will attract and retain an outstanding and dedicated group of capable, creative, and sensitive leaders and the appropriate staff support. Regular assessments of the school's performance and continuing efforts to improve the quality of its programs will be one of the administration's highest priorities.

Implementation:

Action	Responsibility	Initiation Date	Report Date	Completion Date	Resources Needed	Progress
I. Identify the best administrative and staff support system for each division	Headmaster and Heads of School	Underway	Fall '92	Winter '93		
II. Examine administration/teacher hybrid	Administrative Team	Spring '93		Spring '94		
III. Raise administrative salaries to be among highest of I.S.' in area and to 90th percentile of NAIS schools	Trustees Headmaster	Winter '93	Annual	1996	$ from operating budget	
IV. Implement evaluation system for administrators	Headmaster	Fall '92		On-going		
V. Increase use of technology for administrative use	Business	Underway		On-going	$ and training	

145

Shaping Strategy

8. *Governance Goal:*

The Board of Trustees will be composed of a broad range of diverse and talented individuals who represent a balance of expertise, experience, and constituencies. Election to and membership on the Board shall require visible dedication to the school and a commitment to share wisdom, work, and/or wealth in pursuit of the mission and goals of the school.

Implementation: Action	Responsibility	Initiation Date	Report Date	Completion Date	Resources Needed	Progress
I. Educate trustees more fully about the nature of independent education and operations of GA	Committee on Trustees, Chair of Board, Headmaster	Underway	Annual	Spring '93 Formal written program		
II. Continue joint faculty/trustee meetings and trustee/faculty committee work	Chair of Board, Headmaster	Underway	Annual	On-going		
III. Recruit trustees from outside the GA community	Committee on Trustees, Chair of Board, Headmaster	Spring '93		On-going		
IV. Resolve issue of full faculty membership on Board	Board of Trustees	Underway		Spring '92		
V. Actively involve every trustee in raising money for the school	Development Council, Head of Board	Spring '92	Annual	On-going		
VI. Lengthen terms for parent representative from 1 to 2 years	Committee on Trustees	Underway		Winter '92		
VII. Plan ahead for succession of Board leadership	Officers of Board	Underway		On-going		
VIII. Develop candidates for Board by assessing performance on Board committees	Committee Chairpersons	Spring '92	Annual	On-going		

Appendix B

9. *Finances Goal:*

Germantown Academy will be committed to sound financial planning. In its financial planning, the school will balance the competing needs for increased compensation, need-based financial aid, general operating costs, specific program expenses, plant maintenance, and affordable tuitions. It will exercise fiscal discipline in all areas.

Implementation:

Action	Responsibility	Initiation Date	Report Date	Completion Date	Resources Needed	Progress
I. Do 3-5 year financial plan	Finance Committee	Fall '92	Spring '93	Fall '93		
II. Investigate ways to make GA more affordable to the middle class	Admissions and Finance Committees	Fall '92	Spring '93	On-going		
III. Study the long term impact of faculty/staff full tuition remission for faculty/staff hired in the future	Personnel Committee	Spring '92	Fall '92	Winter '92		
IV. Strengthen the summer programs and the auxiliary enterprises of school	Headmaster and Director of Special Programs, Finance Committee	Underway	Spring '92	On-going		
V. Develop and enforce policy of tuition payment	Finance Committee and Director of Finance	Underway	Annual	On-going		
VI. Explore alternative tuition models (part of 3- to 5 yr. financial plan)	Finance Committee and Headmaster	Fall '92	Spring '93	On-going		

10. Development Goal:

Germantown Academy will be committed to the development of financial resources, other than tuition, to fulfill the mission of the school and to fund the goals of the Strategic Plan. The school will seek funds through annual and capital giving to meet the needs for financial aid, merit scholarships, higher salaries and benefits, rising operating costs, specific program expenses, plant maintenance, and debt arising from past capital expenditures.

Implementation: Action	Responsibility	Initiation Date	Report Date	Completion Date	Resources Needed	Progress
I. Increase total annual giving from all sources to 6 percent of the operating budget	Development Office	Fall '92	Annual	Fall '94		
II. Initiate a feasibility study for a possible campaign	Development Office, Development Council and Headmaster	Fall '92		Spring '93		
III. Develop relationships with foundations and corporations	Development Office	Underway	Annual	On-going		
IV. Build a sound database with computer technology	Development Office	Underway	Semi-Annual	On-going		
V. Develop planned giving program	Development Office	Summer '92	Annual	On-going		
VI. Engage a significantly larger percentage of all constituencies in fundraising for school	Development Office	Underway	Annual	On-going		

Appendix B

11. *Alumni Goal:*

Germantown Academy will appreciate its alumni as a critical constituency and cultivate a mutually beneficial relationship with them.

Implementation:

Action	Responsibility	Initiation Date	Report Date	Completion Date	Resources Needed	Progress
I. Increase involvement of alumni in friend and fundraising	Development Office and Alumni Board	Underway	Annual	On-going		
II. Develop programs to bring alumni back to campus	Development Office and Alumni Board	Underway	Annual	On-going		
III. Publication of updated Alumni Directory every 5 years	Development Office			Every 5 yrs.		
IV. Develop in U.S. school students an understanding of future responsibilities as alumni	Development Office and Alumni Board	Underway		On-going		
V. Increase alumni participation in Annual Giving to 40% of alumni	Development Office	Underway	Annual	'93-'94		
VI. Increase alumni giving to make up 1/4 of total Annual Giving	Development Office	Underway	Annual	'93-'94		
VII. Increase involvement of faculty in alumni activities	Development Office	Underway	Annual	On-going		

Shaping Strategy

12. *Physical Plant Goal:*

Germantown Academy enjoys the benefit of an excellent physical plant and will strive to maintain its facilities in a manner that contributes to the success of our overall goals.

Implementation:

Action	Responsibility	Initiation Date	Report Date	Completion Date	Resources Needed	Progress
I. Fund long-term maintenance account on annual basis	Finance Committee, Headmaster	Underway		On-going	Money in annual budget	
II. Evaluate benefits of and increased use of plant by outside groups	Plant Comm. Finance Comm.	Fall '92	Winter '92	Spring '93		
III. Review policies regarding rental use of facilities	Finance Comm. and Plant Comm.	Fall '92	Winter '92	Spring '93		
IV. Study the feasibility of full internal and external access for the physically challenged	Plant and Finance Committee	Spring '93	Spring '95		Part of capital campaign effort	
V. Study maintenance and clean-up requirements and hire sufficient staff to meet them	Director of Finance and Director of Facilities	Fall '92	Winter '92	Spring '93		
VI. Heighten awareness of environmental concerns	Plant Comm. and Student Run Organization	Fall '92	Annual	On-going		
VII. Ensure all federal, state, and local guidelines are met with reference to campus	Plant Comm.	Fall '92	Winter '92	Spring '93		
VIII. Study food service	Director of Finance	Fall '92	Winter '92	Spring '93		

Appendix C

Sample Implementation Program
St. Martin's Episcopal School
Metairie, Louisiana

Implementation Program
St. Martin's Episcopal School

Policy Goal:

1. **Program:** St. Martin's will continue its tradition of academic excellence and will offer a college preparatory program designed to develop strong academic skills, the ability to communicate effectively, and the capacity to work both cooperatively and independently. St. Martin's will continue to base its program on the appreciation of knowledge and analytical thought, the values of the Christian faith, and the historic principles of freedom and democracy.

Short Term Goals:

Action	Responsibility	Initiation Date	Report Date	Resources Needed	Approval/Authority	Overall Appraisal
1. Curriculum Review: Annual Review of course offerings. Courses descriptions – outlining goals to be accomplished by the end of the school year and teaching styles to be utilized.	LS Head/Pre K-3 4-12 Dept. Ch., English, Math, Science, Foreign Language, History. To be visited - F/90, Fine Arts, Athletics, Libraries.	8/89	9/90	Operating Budget	Div. Head	Asst. Head AAC
2. Implementation of Middle School Computer Program. Review the use of the computers as teaching tools. Make written recommendations for changes.	Comp. Com.	8/90	5/91	Operating Budget	MS Head	Head/Asst. AAC
3. Review College Counseling Program. Prepare a written report outlining needs and recommendations for change.	US Head Asst. Head	6/90	1/91	None	Asst. Head	Head
4. Review present SAT/PSAT/ACT Prep. program and make recommendations for changes in a written report.	Asst. Head US Head	7/90	1/91	Operating Budget	US Head	Asst. Head
5. Increase student participation in the Fine Arts. Make recommendations for necessary program or schedule changes.	Div. Heads Fine Arts Fac.	8/90	4/91	Operating Budget	Div. Heads	US Head MS Head Fine Arts Fac.
6. Review present co-curricular and extra-curricular programs and make recommendations for increased student participation and responsibility.	Div. Heads	8/90	1/91	Operating Budget	Div. Head	Div. Heads

Appendix C

Short Term Goals: (continued)

Action	Responsibility	Initiation Date	Report Date	Resources Needed	Approval/ Authority	Overall Appraisal
7. Study the present foreign language requirements of competitive colleges and report real and potential alterations.	For. Lang. Fac.	9/90	2/91	College Counselor	US Head	Asst. Head/ For. Lang. Dept. Ch.
8. Investigate the possibility of offering a Math/Science Camp during the summer – open to public.	Fac./Dir. Dev.	5/90	12/90	Implementation may require budgetary decisions.	Asst. Head	Head
9. Review and recommend changes to insure a comprehensive physical education and athletic program.	Ath.Dir. P.E. Fac.	8/90	6/91	None	Div. Heads	Head

Long Term Goals:

Action	Responsibility	Initiation Date	Completion Date	Resources Needed	Approval/ Authority	Overall Appraisal
1. Study potential for foreign language offerings in the 6th grade and in the Lower School.	Dept. Ch. For. Lang. Fac.		10/92	Implementation may require budgetary decision.	Asst. Head	Head Dept. Ch.
2. Study the need for a child care program. Evaluate information received on Parent Survey and assess parental interest through follow up surveys and unsolicited requests.	LS Head/Adm.		5/92	Implementation may require budgetary decision.	Head/Board Bus. Aff.	Head
3. Study potential of lengthening the school year.	Head/Asst. Head		5/92	Operating Budget	Head/Board	Head Asst. Head
4. Three-year cycle of evaluations for Departments and Divisions.	Head/AAC		9/92	Operating Budget	Asst. Head	Asst. Head AAC

Shaping Strategy

Policy Goal:

2. Faculty: St. Martin's will continue to recognize and support the professional standing, dignity, and growth of the faculty and will provide competitive forms and levels of compensation in order to attract and retain talented, experienced, and diverse faculty who embrace the philosophy of the school.

Short Term Goals:

Action	Responsibility	Initiation Date	Report Date	Resources Needed	Approval/ Authority	Overall Appraisal
1. Adopt and implement revised faculty evaluation process.	Fac. Com.	9/90	11/90	Operating Budget	Div. Heads	Head/Fac. Com.
2. Develop a clear sense of the mission of the school among the faculty and their role in it.	Head/Div. Heads	8/90	6/91	None	Div. Heads	Head/Div. Heads
3. Investigate pay programs of similar NAIS schools. Recommend a program which rewards excellence in teaching and assures competitive salaries.	Fac. Benefits Com.	10/89	12/90	Operating Budget	Head	Head/Fac. Com.
4. Annually review and evaluate benefits for faculty and recommend changes.	Fac. Benefits Com.	10/89	12/90	Implementation may require budgetary decisions.	Head/BOT Bus. Aff.	Head/Fac. Com.
5. Investigate innovative ways to support and recognize faculty and staff efforts and recommendations.	Exec. Com. Parent Groups	9/90	5/91	Implementation may require budgetary decisions.	Head/BOT AAC	Exec. Com.
6. Develop a faculty awareness program to encourage application toward grant opportunities, continuing education, and seminars.	Asst. Head	9/90	12/90	Operating Budget	Asst. Head	Head

Long Term Goals:

			Completion Date			
1. Increase salary levels of faculty to a comparable level of similar ISAS Schools.	Head/BOT Bus. Aff.		2/93	Budgetary Decisions	Board	Head/BOT Bus. Aff.
2. To raise an endowment of $250,000 to support a faculty development program which would include faculty sabbaticals.	BOT/Dev. Com.		9/93	Dev. Office Support	Board	Dev. Com.

Appendix C

Policy Goal:

3. **Students:** St. Martin's will attract promising students of diverse backgrounds who will be actively involved, supportive, and respectful of their fellow students. The student body will be of a size to allow for the development and continuation of broad program offerings founded upon academic excellence. Students will be encouraged to excel academically and at the same time to contribute generously to the full range of school life.

Short Term Goals:

Action	Responsibility	Initiation Date	Report Date	Resources Needed	Approval/ Authority	Overall Appraisal
1. Evaluate admissions policy and procedures and make changes as needed.	Adm. Dept. BOT Adm. Com.	10/90	12/90	Operating Budget	Head/BOT	Adm. Dir. BOT Adm. Com.
2. Develop a minimum student population model which will allow the school to operate without significant alteration to program.	Head/Bus. Mgr.	9/90	12/90	Operating Budget	Head	Head/Bus. Mgr.
3. Confirm the school's commitment to diversification – parent meetings, *Bell* articles, parent newsletter.	Head/E.C. BOT Adm. Com.	9/90	5/91	Operating Budget	Head	BOT Adm. Com.
4. Develop a recruiting program among our parents and alumni to identify potential candidates – from professional families of color.	Adm. Dept.	9/90	12/90	Operating Budget/ Dev. Office	Adm. Dir.	Head
5. Increase student involvement in academic and extra curricular competitions.	Div. Heads Fac.	9/90	5/91	Operating Budget	Div. Heads	Div. Heads
6. Review present procedures for increasing student retention rate and develop new methods.	E.C./Head	9/90	1/91	Operating Budget	Head	Head/Div. Heads

Long Range Goals:

			Completion Date			
1. Translate the minimum student population model into sizing criteria to be utilized in admissions/retention decisions.	Head/Div. Head		11/91	Operating Budget	Head	Head/Div. Head
2. To raise an endowment of $2,500,000 to support financial aid to non-faculty children.	BOT/Dev. Com.		9/95	Dev. Office	Board	BOT Dev. Com.

155

Shaping Strategy

Policy Goal:

4. Parents: St. Martin's will encourage active parental involvement in the school in order to develop a greater understanding of and commitment to the philosophy and programs of the school.

Short Term Goals:

Action	Responsibility	Initiation Date	Report Date	Resources Needed	Approval/ Authority	Overall Appraisal
1. Consider methods to communicate the school's mission and the school's expectations for its students to the parents while concurrently defining their role.	Head Div. Heads	8/90	6/90	None	Head	Head Div. Heads
2. Provide for individual parent conferences to be held on every grade level with advisors and/or division heads.	Div. Head	9/90	2/90	Operating Budget	Div. Heads	Div. Heads
3. Study present methods used to inform parents about the school program and recommend changes about those methods.	Div. Head Dev. Dir.	9/90	10/91	None	Div. Heads Dev. Dir.	Head/E.C.
4. Develop a system where each divisional office is manned at all times during the school day.	Div. Head	2/90	10/90	Operating Budget	Div. Heads.	Div. Heads
5. Initiate breakfast meetings for parents with headmaster – an open forum to share concerns and promote the school's programs and needs.	Head Dev. Dir	8/90	11/91	Operating Budget	Head	Head Dev. Dir.
6. Re-establish parent support groups in conjunction with the Parent Symposium.	Asst. Head	7/90	10/91	Operating Budget	Asst. Head	E.C.

Long Term Goals:

			Completion Date			
1. Develop a data base of parent expertise to be used by faculty and staff as an enrichment resource in class and other school related activities.	Mother's Club Dad's Club Dev. Dir		9/91	Operating Budget/ Dev. Office	Dev. Dir.	Head
2. Increase parent participation in Annual Giving to 80%.	Dev. Dir.		6/93	Operating Budget	Dev. Dir.	Head

Appendix C

Policy Goal:

5. Alumni: St. Martin's will continue to recognize its alumni as a vital and integral constituency and encourage their active involvement in the school.

Short Term Goals:

Action	Responsibility	Initiation Date	Report Date	Resources Needed	Approval/ Authority	Overall Appraisal
1. Increase the involvement and activities of the Alumni Board and alumni in school related activities – i.e. Homecoming, Brown Bag Lunches, Spirits Party, reunions, special honors, etc.	Dev. Dir. Adm. Dir.	8/90	11/90	Possible Budgetary Decisions	Dev. Dir. Adm. Dir.	Head
2. Reintroduce the career day concept.	US Head	9/90	11/90	Operating Budget	US Head	US Head Dev. Dir.
3. Annually review the admissions policy and procedures with regard to alumni.	Head Adm. Office	9/90	10/90	None	Head	Head/ Adm. Office

Long Term Goals:

Action	Responsibility	Completion Date	Resources Needed	Approval/ Authority	Overall Appraisal
1. Develop an alumni base which would include occupational information.	Dev. Office	8/92	None	Div. Heads.	Dev. Office
2. Increase Alumni participation in Annual Giving to 50%.	Dev. Office	6/93	Operating Budget	Dev. Dir.	Dev. Office

Shaping Strategy

Policy Goal:

6. Administration: The Headmaster and administrative staff, who are responsible for institutional solidity and philosophical continuity of the school, will articulate and implement board policy in terms of the mission of the school and effectively supervise all school and administrative operations through clearly delineated lines of responsibility.

Short Term Goals:

Action	Responsibility	Initiation Date	Report Date	Resources Needed	Approval/ Authority	Overall Appraisal
1. Annual evaluation of the headmaster by the board.	BOT	5/90	8/90	None	BOT	BOT
2. Annual evaluation of the administration by the headmaster.	Head	9/90	5/91	None	Head	Head
3. Review and revise administrative job descriptions annually.	Head	8/90	10/90	None	Head	Head
4. Annual review of the Long Range Plan with goal setting for school operations – short and long term.	Head/BOT	5/90	9/90	None	BOT	Head/BOT

Long Term Goals:

		Completion Date			
1. Develop a plan for regular professional enrichment to ensure administrative awareness of local and national trends which may affect education in general and at St. Martin's specifically.	Head	8/91	Implementation may require budgetary decisions.	Head/BOT	Head

Appendix C

Policy Goal:

7. **Plant:** St. Martin's will develop and maintain a physical plant designed to support a distinctive college preparatory program. The existing campus with its natural setting and buildings historic to the school will be preserved and enhanced.

Short Term Goals:

Action	Responsibility	Initiation Date	Report Date	Resources Needed	Approval/ Authority	Overall Appraisal
1. Semi-annually prioritize the maintenance needs of the school and attempt to eliminate deferred maintenance – include cost estimates.	Head/Bus. Mgr.	7/90 1/91	10/90 2/91	Operating Budget	Head	Head/Bus. Mgr.
2. Review salary levels of maintenance personnel and make recommendations.	Head	7/90	10/90	None	Head	Bus. Mgr.
3. Annual review of the Long Range Physical Facilities Plant to determine priorities.	Head/BOT Bus. Aff.	9/90	10/90	None	Board	Head/BOT Bus. Aff.
4. Formulate a funding program for construction of proposed capital improvements in the Long Range Physical Plan.	Board Dev. Com.	9/90	3/91	Possible budgetary decisions Dev. Office	Board	BOT Dev. Com.

Long Term Goals:

		Completion Date			
1. Develop a plan which outlines a timetable for preventative maintenance for building and grounds.	Bus. Mgr.	10/91	None	Head/BOT Bus. Aff.	Bus. Mgr.

159

Shaping Strategy

Policy Goal:

8. **Finance and Development:** St. Martin's will maintain financial stability through prudent business practices, careful long-range financial planning, increased endowment funding, and capital and Annual Giving programs.

Short Term Goals:

Action	Responsibility	Initiation Date	Report Date	Resources Needed	Approval/ Authority	Overall Appraisal
1. Develop a written Long Range Financial Plan which includes the minimum student population model.	Head/Bus. Mgr. BOT Bus. Aff.	12/90	8/91	None	Head/BOT	Head/Bus. Mgr./BOT Bus. Aff.
2. Annually coordinate all fund raising activities within the school and the distribution of funds.	Head Dev. Dir.	5/90	10/90	None	Head	Dev. Dir.
3. Increase Annual Giving participation among all constituencies – set dollar goal for annual budget.	Dev. Dir.	5/90	11/90	None	Head	Dev. Dir.
4. Implement Planned Giving Program.	Dev. Dir./BOT Dev. Com.	5/90	10/90	None	Head/BOT	Dev. Dir.
5. Continue to reduce school's indebtedness.	Head/Bus. Aff.		6/91	Operating Budget	BOT	BOT/Bus. Aff.

Long Term Goals:

Action	Responsibility	Completion Date	Resources Needed	Approval/ Authority	Overall Appraisal
1. Increase the school's cash endowment to $5,000,000 – which would include the faculty development and the financial aid goals.	BOT Dev. Com. Dev. Dir.	8/2000	Dev. Offices	BOT	BOT Dev. Com.
2. Eliminate school's indebtedness.	BOT Bus. Aff. BOT Dev. Com. Dev. Dir.	8/95	Dev. Offices	BOT	BOT Bus. Aff. BOT Dev. Com.

Policy Goal:

9. **Marketing and Public Relations:** St. Martin's will promote its commitment to excellence within a Christian environment and all its other traditions, including the ideal of a "family school."

Short Term Goals:

Action	Responsibility	Initiation Date	Report Date	Resources Needed	Approval/ Authority	Overall Appraisal
1. Annual review of publications, promotional materials, and school activities with recommendations to help emphasize the religious character of the school.	Head/Relig. Dept. Dev. Dir.	8/90	11/90	Dev. Office	Head	Head/BOT Christian Life
2. Maintain a high visibility level in the media concerning student, faculty, staff, alumni, and program achievements – monthly report.	Dev. Dir.		10/90	None	Dev. Dir.	Head
3. Annual review of services to our students and families – i.e. transportation, bookstore, cafeteria, etc.	Bus. Mgr./E.C.	8/90	11/90	None	Bus. Mgr.	Head/E.C.
4. Review present methods and investigate new ways to keep our parents informed about the school's regular and unique programs.	Div. Heads/Mother's Dad's Clubs	9/90	12/90	None	Head	Mother's/Dad's Clubs/Div. Head
5. Review present methods and investigate new ways to help our families build a stronger bond with the school.	Div. Heads/Mother's Dad's Clubs	9/90	5/91	None	Head	Div. Heads/ Mother's/Dad's Clubs
6. Study the demographics of N.O. and recommend various groups to be targeted for Admissions.	Adm. Dir./BOT Adm. and Recruitment	8/90	5/91	None	Adm. Dir.	Head/Adm. Dir.
7. Strengthen relationship with sister Episcopal schools through coordinated activities.	Head/Adm. Dir.	8/90	5/91	Implementation may require budgetary decisions.	Head	Head/Adm. Dir

Long Term Goals:

			Completion Date			
1. Develop individual marketing strategies for targeted groups of parents and students.	BOT Adm. Office Adm. Office		10/91	Implementation may require budgetary decisions.	Head/BOT	
2. Strengthen relationship with sister Episcopal schools through coordinated activities.	Head/E.C.		8/92	Implementation may require budgetary decisions.	Head	Head/E.C.

Appendix C

161

Shaping Strategy

Policy Goal:

10. **Board and Governance:** St. Martin's will continue to look to leadership from a diverse, effective, well-informed Board of Trustees who establish policy for the school, support the administration in its implementation of policy, communicate with all constituencies, and evaluate the programs and objectives of the school.

Short Term Goals:

Action	Responsibility	Initiation Date	Report Date	Resources Needed	Approval/ Authority	Overall Appraisal
1. Acquaint the Board of Trustees with one major program development each month.	Head/Fac.	8/90	6/91	None	Head	Head/BOT
2. Inform the Board of local and national educational issues at least three times per year.	Head		6/91	None	Head	BOT
3. Annual self-evaluation of the Board of Trustees.	BOT Pres.		8/90	None	BOT	BOT
4. Annual review of the process made of implementing the Long Range Plan and in setting new implementation plans for the following year.	Head/BOT		9/90	None	BOT	Head/BOT
5. Review Long Range Plan and develop a plan for recruiting potential Board of Trustees.	BOT Pres. BOT E.C.	8/90	11/90	None	BOT	BOT
6. Review present and recommend new training programs for new members of the Board of Trustees.	Head/BOT Pres.	8/90	12/90	None	BOT	BOT
7. Develop a Board Policy Handbook.	BOT Com. Ch. BOT Sec.	8/90	10/90	None	BOT	BOT BOT Pres.
8. Encourage Board of Trustees involvement in the financial affairs and fund raising efforts of the school.	BOT Pres.	8/90	6/91	None	BOT	BOT

Appendix D

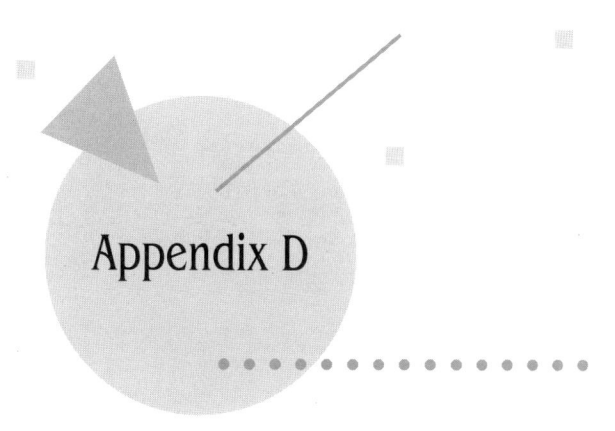

Sample Computerized Implementation Program

Mary Institute
St. Louis, Missouri

This implementation program could be sorted by time sequence, topic, and individual responsibility. It is printed here with thanks to Susan Elliott, who designed the program when she was a trustee at Mary Institute.

Shaping Strategy

Mary Institute
Long Range Planning

Policy Goal:

Marketing: Mary Institute will expand and intensify its promotional activities on a broad scale, in order to ensure a thriving student applicant pool, enhance the School's competitive edge in hiring outstanding faculty and administration, achieve the widest and deepest possible constituent community loyalty, and provide for students and graduates a high degree of support and cause for pride in Mary Institute.

Action	Responsibility	Initiation Date	Progress Report Date	Completion Date	Approval/ Authority	Overall Appraisal
1. Create a Board level Marketing/PR/Communications committee to work closely with the administration in furthering the School's vital interests.	Exec. Cts. BOT					
2. Develop a long range marketing plan based on sound understanding of current and anticipated market dynamics, challenges and opportunities.	Adm. Dir. Headmaster BOT	2/86	4/86	6/86	Mkt./PR Cts. Exec. Cts. Headmaster BOT	Annual
3. Devise specific marketing strategies to achieve goals set for size and composition of the School's population.	Adm. Dir. Mkt./PR Cts.	3/86	4/86	6/86	Mkt./PR Cts. Exec. Cts. Headmaster BOT	Semi-Annual
4. Review current information and processes of Mary Institute and Ronald S. Beasley School.	Adm. Dir. Comm. Dir. Headmaster		2/86	2/86	Mkt./PR Cts.	Annual
5. Design new materials and dissemination processes for information to specific mkts: community, new applicant prospects, current and former parents and grandparents, alums, business, real estate leaders, staff.	Mkt./PR Ch. Adm. Dir.		4/86		Mkt./PR Cts. Headmaster BOT	On-going
6. Develop program of regular statistical analysis of market demographics and admissions activity. *Phase I.*	Adm. Dir. Headmaster		2/86	3/86	Adm. Dir. Headmaster	On-going

(continued)

Appendix D

Policy Goal: (continued)

Action	Responsibility	Initiation Date	Progress Report Date	Completion Date	Approval/ Authority	Overall Appraisal
7. Develop program of regular surveys to understand perceptions of Mary Institute program with various audiences.	Adm. Dir. Outside Pros.		2/86	3/86	Mkt./PR Cts. Headmaster Exec. Cts.	2-3 years
8. Develop programs to use educational contacts, national and local, to promote School among professionals. *Phase II.*	Adm. Dir. Mkt./PR Cts. Adm. Headmaster		3/86		Mkt./PR Cts. Adm. Dir. Headmaster	On-going
9. Develop programs that help parents and alumnae play a strong role in enhancing the community's response to the School. *Phase II.*	Adm. Dir. Mkt./PR Cts. Comm. Dir. Parents/Alum. Assn.		2/86		Adm. Dir. Headmaster BOT	On-going
	Adm. Dir. Headmaster BOT	2/86	4/86	6/86	Mkt./Pr. Cts. Exec. Cts. Headmaster BOT	Annual

165

Notes

Notes

Notes